THE BE

THE

2017

"An authority acknowledged even by the Champenois ..." **The Sunday Times**

a **PS** book

THE BEST FIZZ ON THE PLANET 2017

Tom Stevenson

This paperback edition has been published under the PS Book imprint by Price-Sinclair Publishing

TASTING NOTES in this 2017 edition are based on a compilation of notes written by Tom Stevenson, Essi Avellan MW, Dr Tony Jordan & George Markus at THE CHAMPAGNE & SPARKLING WINE WORLD CHAMPIONSHIPS 2016
CSWWC COMPETITION VENUE Salomons Estate, Tunbridge Wells
CSWWC COMPETITION RESIDENCE Hotel du Vin, Tunbridge Wells
CSWWC COMPETITION GLASSES Riedel Vinum Chianti (6416/15)
CSWWC COMPETITION JUDGES Tom Stevenson, Essi Avellan MW, Dr Tony Jordan
CSWWC PERMANENT RESERVE JUDGE George Markus
CSWWC COMPETITION STEWARD Simon Stockton
CSWWC TASTING QUALITY CONTROL Orsi Szentkiralyi
CSWWC COMPETITION LOGISTICS Karl Franz of Sensible Wine Services
ART DIRECTOR Michael Foyle
CSWWC FINANCE Eva Callaghan
CSWWC PR Madamé Bryony Wright
CSWWC PA TO TOM STEVENSON Princess Rachel Davey
ISBN 978-1911351009 (B&W Softback)

Foreword

Welcome to the first edition of *The Best Fizz on the Planet*.

If you are a fizz geek, a wine professional or a wine student looking for the latest and most technically comprehensive guide to sparkling wine, then you should buy my *Champagne & Sparkling Wine Guide*, which not only includes all the best fizz on the planet, but is also updated annually with the latest technical details in the opening chapters and the Micropedia.

However, if you just "drink drink" rather than "drink and think drink", this LITE edition consists of only each year's recommended wines and should be more than enough to keep you up-to-date with the very best Champagnes and sparkling wines to buy.

The wines recommended here (and in the fully-fledged *Champagne & Sparkling Wine Guide*) have all been awarded either a Gold or Silver medal at THE CHAMPAGNE & SPARKLING WINE WORLD CHAMPIONSHIPS, the only competition in the world that is judged exclusively by three leading Champagne & sparkling wine specialists.

Tom Stevenson, December 2016

The Best Fizz on the Planet

To win a medal at THE CHAMPAGNE & SPARKLING WINE WORLD CHAMPIONSHIPS (CSWWC) all wines are tasted and assessed by origin, which is to say that all Proseccos are tasted together, as are all Cavas, English sparkling wines, Australian fizz, Champagnes and so on. This ensures that the potential of each wine is evaluated within the context of its typicity of provenance.

The wines are also tasted by style, such as Brut, Brut Nature, Blend, Blanc de Blancs, Rosé etc. Obviously Pinot Noir produces a different wine than, say, Chardonnay, but it is equally true to say that Pinot Noir grown in New Zealand produces a different type of wine than Pinot Noir grown in England. The typicity of even the most specific style of sparkling wine thus varies according to its provenance. This is why the CSWWC believes it is essential for its medals to be evaluated strictly by origin and style.

Every wine tasted is assessed as Gold, Silver, Bronze, Commended, No Award, Possibly Faulty & Definitely Faulty, but we award and publish only Gold and Silver medals. How any competition classifies a Bronze, it is a third-rate medal by definition. It is not an Olympic Bronze, which is given to the third-best in the world. It is a minor medal churned out by wine competitions in vast numbers, making "Third Class" a better analogy: hard wooden benches if you're lucky, standing room if you're not. Many producers would rather win nothing than be told they have won a Bronze and few wine-lovers go out of their way to buy a Bronze medal wine. As for Commended

For the CSWWC I expect every winning wine to be special and I want consumers to be confident that they are. That is why Bronze medal wines and lower are dumped in the Bin of Shame! Obviously Gold medal wines are the ultimate accolade, but I would be proud to serve a Silver medal wine, not just from the CSWWC but any competition I have judged at. I would be happy to open a Silver medal wine for guests, however knowledgeable they might be. However, we go one level higher for Deluxe Champagnes. All other sparkling wines, Champagnes or not, are winners at the CSWWC if they pick up a Gold or a Silver, but for a Deluxe Champagne we expect nothing less than Gold medal quality. Deluxe Champagnes demand a very high premium and so do we!

The CSWWC is the toughest sparkling wine competition in the world. It provides both consumers and trade with a definitive annual guide to the very best fizz on the planet ... the *Champagne & Sparkling Wine Guide* is that definitive annual guide and *The Best Fizz on the Planet* is a LITE wine-only version.

The Best in Class

All the wines in the competition are initially evaluated by origin and style. This ensures that the medal potential of each wine is evaluated according to its own typicity of provenance, not some international yardstick. Within each category of origin, the wines are assessed by style (e.g. all the Brut Nature together, all the Blanc de Blancs, Rosé etc.). Where no gold medals are awarded, no wine of that style and provenance can progress any further in the competition, but where there are gold medal winners, they are grouped together to find the Best in Class. We also take this opportunity to demote any golds that do not stand shoulder-to-shoulder with the golds won in other flights of the same class.

AUSTRALIA

House of Arras 2006 Blanc de Blancs
Best Australian Blanc de Blancs

House of Arras NV A by Arras
Best Australian NV Blend
Best Value Australian Sparkling Wine

Jansz Tasmania NV Premium Rosé
Best Australian NV Rosé

Chandon 2005 Prestige Cuvée
Best Australian Vintaged Blend

House of Arras 2006 Rosé
Best Australian Vintaged Rosé

CHILE

Santa Digna Estelado Rosé NV Uva Païs
Best Chilean Rosé
Best Chilean Organic

CHINA

Chandon NV Brut Rosé
Best Chinese Rosé

ENGLAND

Wiston Estate 2010 Blanc de Blancs
Best English Blanc de Blancs

Hattingley Valley 2011 Blanc de Blancs
Best English Future Release

Ridgeview 2009 Rosé de Noirs (Magnum)
Best English Magnum

Plumpton Estate NV The Dean Brut
Best English NV Blend

Plumpton Estate NV The Dean Blush
Best English NV Rosé

Squerryes 2011 Brut
Best English Vintaged Blend

Hattingley Valley 2013 Rosé
Best English Vintaged Rosé

FRANCE

Gremillet Blanc de Noirs NV Blanc de Noirs
Best Champagne Blanc de Noirs

Moët & Chandon 1998 Grand Vintage Collection
Best Champagne Future Release (re-release)

Charles Heidsieck 1989 Brut Jeroboam (300cl)
Best Champagne Library Vintage

Ruinart NV Blanc de Blancs (Magnum)
Best Champagne NV Blanc de Blancs
Best Champagne NV Magnum

Charles Heidsieck NV Brut Réserve
Best Champagne NV Blend

Barnaut Authentique NV Grand Cru Rosé
Best Champagne NV Rosé
Best Grower Champagne

Louis Roederer 2010 Blanc de Blancs Brut
Best Champagne Vintaged Blanc de Blancs

Moët & Chandon 2006 Grand Vintage (Magnum)
Best Champagne Vintaged Blend
Best Champagne Vintaged Magnum

Louis Roederer 2010 Brut Rosé
Best Champagne Vintaged Rosé

Taittinger Comtes de Champagne 2006 Blanc de Blancs Brut
Best Deluxe Champagne Blanc de Blancs

Louis Roederer 2002 Cristal Brut (Magnum)
Best Deluxe Champagne Blend
Best Deluxe Champagne Magnum
Best Deluxe Champagne

Dom Pérignon Rosé 1995 P2
Best Deluxe Champagne Library Vintage

Louis Roederer 2002 Cristal Brut Rosé (Magnum)
Best Deluxe Champagne Rosé

Bouvet Saumur Saphir 2013 Brut
Best Loire Blend

Devaux NV Ultra D (Magnum)
Best Low or No Dosage Champagne

Pommery Les Clos Pompadour Mis en Cave 2003 (Magnum)
Best Single Vineyard Champagne

Waitrose 2005 Special Réserve Vintage
Best Supermarket Champagne
Best Value Champagne

HUNGARY

Kreinbacher 2011 Brut Classic (Magnum)
Best Hungarian Blanc de Blancs
Best Hungarian Magnum

ITALY

Fratelli Berlucchi Freccianera 2012 Satèn
Best Franciacorta Future Release

Biondelli NV Brut (Magnum)
Best Franciacorta NV Blanc de Blancs
Best Value Franciacorta

Berlucchi '61 NV Brut
Best Franciacorta NV Blend

Berlucchi '61 NV Rosé (Magnum)
Best Franciacorta NV Rosé
Best Franciacorta Magnum

Lantieri 2011 Arcadia Millesimato Brut
Best Franciacorta Vintaged Brut Blend

Uberti 2008 Comarì del Salem (Magnum)
Best Low or No Dosage Franciacorta

Nino Franco 2015 Primo Franco
Best Prosecco Dry

Tenuta Degli Ultimi 2013 Rive di Collalto Biancariva
Best Prosecco Low or No Dosage

Nino Franco NV Rustico
Best Prosecco NV Brut

Nino Franco 2015 Vigneto della Riva di San Floriano
Best Prosecco Vintaged Brut

Madame Martis 2006 Rare Vintage
Best Trentodoc Blend

Ferrari 2007 Riserva Lunelli
Best Trentodoc Low or No Dosage

Ferrari NV Brut (Magnum)
Best Trentodoc NV Blanc de Blancs
Best Trentodoc Magnum

Rotari Rosé NV Brut Rosé (exclusively Italian off-trade)
Best Trentodoc NV Rosé
Best Value Trentodoc

Ferrari 2008 Perlé Brut (Magnum)
Best Trentodoc Vintaged Blanc de Blancs

Rotari Alperegis 2011 Rosé
Best Trentodoc Vintaged Rosé

NEW ZEALAND

No 1 Assemblé NV Brut
Best New Zealand NV Brut Blend

Hunter's Mirumiru™ NV Rosé
Best New Zealand Rosé

Hunter's Mirumiru™ 2011 Reserve
Best New Zealand Vintaged Brut Blend

SOUTH AFRICA

Graham Beck 2009 Cuvée Clive
Best South African Brut Blend

SPAIN

Juvé y Camps Cinta Púrpura 2012 Brut Reserva
Best Cava Future Release

Vilarnau NV Brut Reserva
Best Cava NV Brut Blend

1+1=3 2014 Brut Rosé
Best Cava Rosé

Mas Codina 2013 Brut Reserva
Best Cava Vintaged Blend

Segura Viudas NV Gran Cuvée Reserva
Best Low or No Dosage Cava

UNITED STATES

Roederer Estate NV Brut (Magnum)
Best California Brut Blend

Roederer Estate NV Brut Rosé (Magnum)
Best California Rosé
Best California Magnum

The Best in Region

We taste all the Best in Class to find the Best in Region. **However, if a region does not win any gold medals, no Regional Champion can be awarded.**

CAVA
1+1=3 2014 Brut Rosé

CHAMPAGNE
Louis Roederer 2002 Cristal Brut (Magnum)

LOIRE
Bouvet Saumur Saphir 2013 Brut

FRANCIACORTA
Berlucchi '61 NV Rosé (Magnum)

PROSECCO
Nino Franco NV Rustico

TRENTODOC
Ferrari NV Brut (Magnum)

The National Champions

If there are no recognised sparkling wine regions, the Best in Class from each country compete with one another for a National Champion trophy, the highest *terroir* award in the competition. If there are recognised sparkling wine regions, then it will be the Best in Regions and any unattached Best in Class that will compete. **However, if a country does not win any gold medals, no National Champion trophy can be awarded.**

BEST AUSTRALIAN SPARKLING WINE

Chandon 2005 Prestige Cuvée

Yarra Valley, South Australia, Australia (75cl, 13.20%)
56% Chardonnay, 36% Pinot Noir, 8% Meunier (5g RS)
The pedigree of this wine was obvious to at least one of the judges, who wrote "Classic Moët gunpowder: is this a Chandon?" Superbly toasty, beautiful charred and exuberantly fruity nose. Voluptuous, round and succulent, with a soft, long and lovely, creamy finish. [While Tasmania might possess the most sought after sparkling wine vineyards in Australia and that small island deservedly won the Best Australian Sparkling Wine trophy last year, Chandon 2005 Prestige Cuvée makes the point that there other exciting fizz areas in the country, as it is composed from grapes grown in the Strathbogie Ranges, the Yarra Valley itself, Macedon, King Valley and, inevitably, Tasmania.]

BEST CHILEAN SPARKLING WINE

Santa Digna Estelado Rosé NV Uva Paìs

Secano Interior, Central Valley, Chile (75cl, 12%)
100% Paìs (8g RS)
Exquisitely pale peach colour, elegantly restrained nose, with cool, linear strawberry fruit on the palate finishing with an attractive lemony bite. [Produced by Torres Chile in association with a group of Fairtrade growers called 'Esperanza de la Costa', which is led by the redoubtable

Señora Secundina, a legendary figure who works with País vines that are 150 to 200 years old. The vines harvested for this wine are, however, "only" 80 years old.]

BEST CHINESE SPARKLING WINE

Chandon NV Brut Rosé

Helan Mountain's East Foothills, Ningxia, China (75cl, 12.50%)

70% Chardonnay, 30% Pinot Noir (9g RS)

A medium-deep cherry pink colour is followed by a stylishly fragrant nose of red cherry vibrancy and an attractive toasty undertone. Firm, with a soft and spicy palate, it has a long, well-balanced, true Brut finish. This is not only the best Chinese sparkling wine we have tasted, but also the best Asian sparkling wine by some distance, despite the youthfulness of the operation. [Domaine Chandon China was established in 2013 and released its first sparkling wine in 2014. In addition to a fully operational winery and cellars, it is equipped with technical tasting rooms and a visitor centre.]

BEST ENGLISH SPARKLING WINE

Squerryes 2011 Brut

South Downs, England (75cl, 12%)

100% Chardonnay (8g RS)

What lovely, satisfying, linear wine this is. Bright fruit aromas, fine, focused yeast-complexed fruit on the palate, which is as clean as a whistle, with a lovely, fluffy mousse and a laser-like finish. It is fair to say that we were all totally surprised by the National Trophy result as soon as we discovered its identity, but we were equally as pleased as punch that yet another new English sparkling wine name has hit the heights. [Produced from grapes grown on Squerryes Estate, part of the magnificent, picture-pretty 17th century Squerryes Court, which has been owned by the Warde family since 1731. Squerryes Estate is a single vineyard wine from a chalk escarpment with a flinty-clay topsoil on the North Downs, within the M25 and only 20 miles from central London.]

BEST FRENCH SPARKLING WINE

Louis Roederer 2002 Cristal Brut (Magnum)

Champagne, France (150cl, 12.50%)

55% Pinot Noir, 45% Chardonnay (10G RS%)

Absolute class, so fine and refined with an endless, creamy, tapering finish. The fruit is plush, succulent and juicy, yet its perfect balance and long, linear line provides such finesse. The fruit is so vital and seductive, supported by a mousse creams and puns in the mouth. There is a sense of grace and stature to this Champagne, and a sense of glacial evolution that knocks years off of its chronological age, this surely must be made from the finest raw materials under the guiding influence of one of today's most gifted winemakers. [Produced exclusively from Roederer's Domaine 3, which is reserved for Cristal Brut. This domaine consists of Pinot Noir in the grands crus of Aÿ-Champagne, Beaumont-sur-Vesle, Verzenay, Verzy and a very special premier cru in Mareuil-sur-Aÿ (the lieu-dit of "les Clos", which borders the grand cru of Aÿ and many rate almost as highly), plus Chardonnay from the grands crus of Avize, Cramant and Mesnil-sur-Oger. The difference with 2002 compared to previous Cristal vintages is the increase in oak-fermented components. In the 1990s oak-fermented wines represented just 10-15 per cent of the final Cristal blend, but the oak is large foudres, the effects of which when combined with the battonage on gros lies are always textural, never aromatic.]

BEST HUNGARIAN SPARKLING WINE

Kreinbacher 2011 Brut Classic (Magnum)
Somló, Somló-Hegy, Hungary (150cl, 12%)
100% Furmint (11.1G RS%)
This wine has a bright, lemon-gold colour, a nicely autolytic nose with pastry and toasty richness over opulent fruit of absolutely glacial evolution, and a gorgeous vanilla flick of potential complexity on the finish. Would love to age this anther 3-5 years! [The non-vintage Brut Prestige was a different wine and a different class this year, easily deserving its Gold over the Silver it won in 2015. However, the 2011 Brut Classic, the first vintage cuvée and the first magnum that Kreinbacher has entered, is on a completely different level again. If the Brut Prestige illustrates how quickly Kreinbacher is learning and improving, then the Brut Classic in magnum demonstrates the sparkling wine potential for Furmint, which is something that none of knew until now.]

BEST ITALIAN SPARKLING WINE

Berlucchi '61 NV Rosé (Magnum)
Franciacorta DOCG, Lombardy, Italy (150cl, 12.50%)
40% Chardonnay, 60% Pinot Noir (8G RS%)
Strikingly starbright pale-salmon colour, this wine exudes fine aromatics, with pastry complexity and gunpowder notes. This is a wine that is oozing fruit on the palate, but it is very fine fruit, thanks to the silky finesse of its mousse. Some aged complexity . Very long and sophisticated, with an excellent dry brut finish. Nice acid line adds freshness, vitality and purity. [When we saw the identity of the top Italian sparkling wine, it was a bit of a surprise. Guido Berlucchi is the largest producer in Franciacorta, so it was a bit like awarding Moët NV Rosé Best French Sparkling Wine. When some Italian wine experts see the label, they can be a bit sniffy about Guido Berlucchi, but tasted blind this rosé rocks. It looks smart, it tastes smart, and it is smart. We award medals and trophies according to the quality of the wine, not the volume of its production.]

BEST NEW ZEALAND SPARKLING WINE

Hunter's Mirumiru™ 2011 Reserve

Marlborough, New Zealand (75cl, 12.50%)
55% Pinot Noir, 42% Chardonnay, 3% Meunier (6.7G RS%)
Intense lemon colour, yeasty-toasty complexed aromas followed by lovely fruit that dances on the palate and finishes with a soft creaminess on aftertaste. Intelligent blending and use of malolactic. Nice leesy and autolytic undertone. Crisp and classy palate, with a lovely firm and fruity brut finish. [Judged in the absence of Tony Jordan, who consults for two wineries in New Zealand, including Hunter's, and thus withdrew from judging any of the sparkling wines from this country.]

BEST SOUTH AFRICAN SPARKLING WINE

Graham Beck 2009 Cuvée Clive

Cap Classique, Western Cape, South Africa (75cl, 12.20%)
80% Chardonnay, 20% Pinot Noir (7.4G RS%)
Gunpowder Chardonnay; fine, rich, explosive, as one judge succinctly put it! Medium- lemon colour, with an exuberantly toasty, charred nose, laced with notes of ground coffee and leesy complexity. [Pieter Ferreira, the bubbly Mr Bubble of Cap Classique, returns to pick up the South African national trophy, but not for his Blanc de Blancs, which is widely regarded as consistently the finest Cap Classique produced, but for Cuvée Clive, Graham Beck's relatively new prestige cuvée. The Chardonnay comes from their limestone vineyards in Robertson while the Pinot Noir comes from their vineyard in Firgrove, Stellenbosch. The grapes are whole-bunch pressed, with only the tête de cuvée used. Most of the juice is fermented in stainless steel at 16°C, with a small portion of Chardonnay fermented in authentic oak pièces (205 litres). After bottling the wines are aged on yeast for a minimum of 60 months.]

BEST SPANISH SPARKLING WINE

1+1=3 2014 Brut Rosé

Cava DO, Alt Penedès, Spain (75cl, 11.50%)
80% Grenache, 15% Pinot Noir, 5% Trepat (0.7G RS%)
When critics discuss red and white wines, you may hear mention of "the New Spain". Well, this is "the New Cava" and, specifically "the New Cava Rosado": delicate in colour, fruit and weight. So light, long and fine, fresh, youthful peachy fruit and long, soft, linear finish. Crisp and zesty, with a lovely freshness and easiness to it. [The find of CSWWC 2016! I discovered this wine on a recent trip to Penedès and immediately asked for it to be added to a masterclass I was giving in Barcelona the next day. It was then entered into the CSWWC where I was happy to discover that my fellow judges were equally impressed. Readers might think that 1+1=3 refers to an assemblage where the final product is superior to the sum of its parts,

but in fact it refers to the owners, winemaker Josep Pinol and viticulturist Josep Bonnell, brothers-in-law who believe they work better together than apart.]

BEST US SPARKLING WINE

Roederer Estate NV Brut Rosé (Magnum)
Anderson Valley AVA, California, USA (150cl, 12%)
45% Chardonnay, 55% Pinot Noir (12G RS%)
A beautifully pale pink-peach colour. Classy yeast-complexed, toasty-gunflint nose, with bright, gorgeously exuberant fruitiness on a linear palate with a sumptuous mousse and an exquisite acid-line: what more could you ask for? [In 1987 Roederer Estate produced the first sparkling wine outside of Champagne to achieve the quality not simply of an average Champagne, but of a very good Champagne. Its first wine was produced in 1986, but that did not hack it, whereas in 1987, with the benefit of oak-matured reserves from 1986, it did. Nearly a quarter of a century later, this non vintage blend was built around the 2011 harvest, which was not only cool, but also rainier than usual in spring and early autumn. So we have a California sparkling wine made from very European weather collecting the US national trophy.]

World Champions by Style

Every appropriate Best in Class in the competition compete for the title of World Champion in eight select sparkling wine categories (of which only six were awarded this year):

WORLD CHAMPION CLASSIC NV BRUT BLEND
Charles Heidsieck NV Brut Réserve
Champagne, France (75cl, 12.80%)
33% Pinot Noir, 34% Meunier, 33% Chardonnay (11.2G RS%)
This wonderfully toasty Champagne is more like a cellar-aged non-vintage than the current non-vintage blend. Lovely, charred, roasted-coffee aromas with notes of honey and dried-fruit complexity. Calm, concentrated and long. [From the most award-winning Champagne producer on the planet, this specific blend was made by the late Thierry Roset. It was Roset who took the tried and tested Brut Réserve recipe of late, great Daniel Thibault and improved it, even though he reduced the number of crus by half (from 120 to just 60). He achieved this minor miracle by placing more emphasis on Oger (for Chardonnay), Ambonnay (for Pinot Noir) and Verneuil (for Meunier), the three crus that have always been the heart and soul of Thibault's highly acclaimed cuvée. He also introduced a fatter bottle with a narrower neck to reduce oxygen ingress and slow the wine's evolution. He did not alter the percentage of reserve wine (an impressive 40%), but slower evolution allowed him to increase the maximum age of reserves from eight years to between 10 and 15. Winning the World Champion trophy for NV Brut Blend is a fine tribute to Roset, who passed away in 2014 at the relatively young age of 55. It also serves as inspiration for Charles Heidsieck's new chef de caves, Cyril Brun.]

WORLD CHAMPION CLASSIC VINTAGED BRUT BLEND
Moët & Chandon 2006 Grand Vintage (Magnum)
Champagne, France (150cl, 12.50%)
42% Chardonnay, 39% Pinot Noir, 19% Meunier (5G RS%)

Judging is not about guessing. In fact, guessing can play havoc with the supposedly objective task of quality assessment under blind conditions, as it introduces an element of subjective bias. However, the Moët gunpowder style is so alive in this wine that it stood out like firework night for everyone. The aromas are very youthful, despite the gunpowdery sulphidic complexity, and this youthfulness is followed on the palate, which is brimming with lovely, sweet, pure fruitiness that is creamy and caressing, lingering in the gentlest manner. While 2006 might not be a truly great vintage, this magnum of 2006 is without doubt a truly great Champagne. [Produced by the super-talented Benoît Gouez during his second year in full control as chef de caves at Moët, 2006 was the first vintage at this house to benefit from Diam Mytik technical closures, which eliminate TCA.]

WORLD CHAMPION CLASSIC BLANC DE BLANCS BRUT
Ferrari NV Brut (Magnum)
Trentodoc, Trentino Alto Adige, Italy (150cl, 12.50%)
100% Chardonnay (6G RS%)
Autolytic notes over ripe citrus fruit with toast building up. Intense, but not at all weighty, linear fruit, crisp, zesty and full of life. Lovely, tapering length with fine acid line. Voluminous mousse adds creaminess to the finish. Classic Blanc de Blancs. [Last year's Sparkling Wine Producer of the Year was up against serious competition, yet its bog-standard non-vintage – if any wine from Ferrari can be described as bog-standard – ran away with the World Champion Classic Blanc de Blancs Brut trophy. What an achievement.]

WORLD CHAMPION CLASSIC ROSÉ BRUT
Louis Roederer 2010 Brut Rosé
Champagne, France (75cl, 12.50%)
62% Pinot Noir, 38% Chardonnay (9G RS%)
This adorably pale-peach concoction has such lovely, fresh, delicate, fragrant, peachy fruit aromas with such subtle notes of toast and vanilla that they completely mislead the taster, who will expect the palate to be equally delicate and fragrant on the palate, only to be rudely awoken by an explosion of fruit. This is, without doubt, an extremely classy sparkling wine, but its Pinot-dominated fruit is just so very rich that it comes as a bit of a shock! Thankfully the explosion of rich fruit is so succulent and juicy that it enhances the wine's finesse, rather than working against it, and this is further reinforced by the tight, long and lingering finish. [Chef de caves Jean-Baptiste Lecaillon uses a unique method to produce this rosé. The Pinot Noir grapes are from Hautvillers and are cold soaked for just over one week. There is no crushing and no fermentation on the skins as that would extract tannins, which is the last thing he wants. The Pinot Noir juice is drained-off and the more acidic Chardonnay juice is added.

Because the Pinot Noir has been picked for ripeness, it needs the Chardonnay's acidity for balance, of course, but by adding the Chardonnay juice at this stage, its acidity stabilises the colour. The temperature of the blend is then gently increased to encourage the first fermentation, approximately 20 per cent of which is carried out in 9000-liter, well-used French oak foudres.]

WORLD CHAMPION BRUT FROM NON-CLASSIC GRAPE
Santa Digna Estelado Rosé NV Uva Paìs
Secano Interior, Central Valley, Chile (75cl, 12%)
100% Paìs (8g RS)
Exquisitely pale peach colour, elegantly restrained nose, with cool, linear strawberry fruit on the palate finishing with an attractive lemony bite. [I am always being asked what non-Champagne grape varieties might be good for sparkling wine and if any competition in the world should be shining a spotlight on this topic it is the CSWWC. That is why I awarded the first-ever Chairman's Trophy to a Silver medal wine made from the Nebbiolo grape (Cuvage Rosé) and now, with the reintroduction of the World Champion trophies, I have fleshed out the non-classic grape variety to an award in its own right. The winning wine can be any pure varietal classic style (Blanc de Blancs, Blanc de Noirs or Rosé) and Brut includes any wine labelled or technically qualifying as Brut Nature, Extra Brut or Brut. We define a non-classic grape as a variety not traditionally associated with a recognised brut style sparkling wine, such as Chardonnay, Pinot Noir and Meunier are for Champagne; Parellada, Macabeo and Xarel-lo are for Cava, Glera are for Prosecco etc.]

WORLD CHAMPION LIBRARY VINTAGE
Dom Pérignon Rosé 1995 P2
Champagne, France (75cl, 12%)
42% Chardonnay, 58% Pinot Noir (6.5G RS)
Deep copper colour with bronzed highlights. Absolutely beautiful Pinot aromas, with mellow, spiced-cherry complexity and notes of chocolate and forest-floor. Great exuberance of fruit on the palate. Positively vinous, with an intense, vibrant and lingering richness. Firm , muscular and full of life for 20-plus years of age, yet velvet-textured, with great focus and freshness, with a lovely, satisfying brut finish. [P2 is the second phase of development when, according to chef de caves Richard Geoffroy, Dom Pérignon starts to show what it is really made of. He believes there are three windows of opportunity or "plenitudes" when any great Champagne will transcend into a distinctly different personality. For DP, the second plenitude (P2) usually takes place at the age 15-20 years, with at least 12 years in contact with the yeast lees. This is the time when DP is supposed be at its peak of energy and the 1995 rosé certainly demonstrates that. For

collectors who are moving on from the 1993 DPR in their cellars, the 1995 could seem a little disappointing because although it has some mellowness, it is nowhere as mellow and as the mellifluous as the starbright, tangerine-coloured 1993 with its creamy-coffee fruit, but that's because the 1993 was more like a P3 when it was launched as a P2, whereas the 1995 is just bursting with life, and that is the quality that makes it such an easy w inner of the Library Vintage Trophy.]

Special Trophies

Before revealing the Supreme World Champion for 2016, there are two awards that deserve special attention: the Chairman's Trophy and Sparkling Wine Producer of the Year.

CHAIRMAN'S TROPHY

In the judging I have no more power than any of the other judges, but after the judging, the Chairman's Trophy is in my gift. It can be for anything I want, for any reason I care to express. Last year the Chairman's Trophy was awarded to the pure Nebbiolo Cuvage for being the most promising classic-style sparkling wine produced from a non-classic grape. The classic wine from non-classic grape concept proved so popular that it is now the theme for its own World Champion by Style trophy. What wine has this year's Chairman's Trophy has been awarded to and why? It is for one of the single-most most outstanding wines in the entire competition. If it is so outstanding, why award it the Chairman's Trophy when it must already be heaped in glory? The truth is that is not heaped in any glory. Why? Because it's a one-off that does not qualify for any Best in Class category, therefore could not be awarded any of the recognised trophies. I scored this Champagne 20 out of 20 and wrote just one word "Wow!" only to discover after the competition that it was unable to progress beyond its Gold medal as it was literally in a class of its own. If we had a Library Multi-Vintage Champagne with very demanding criteria, it could I suppose have won that, but as only one wine in the world could possibly qualify for such a category, that's not going to happen (unless the winner inspires other producers to create a serious category for such wines). It would have been a disgrace if such a brilliantly crafted Champagne as MCIII did not receive one of the top prizes at a niche competition like the CSWWC. The was never any doubt who the winner of the Chairman's Trophy should be in 2016 ...

MCIII by Moët & Chandon 001.14
Champagne, France (75cl, 12.50%)
45% Pinot Noir, 45% Chardonnay, 10% Meunier (5G RS%)
An absolutely spellbinding blend of great reserve wines. Immaculate. Full-on soft, spicy, complex aromas of apricot, meadow flowers and honey with evolved pastry notes. Lovely spiciness, very complex, overflowing with reserve wine mellowness and richness, caressed by the beautiful, velvety sweetness of mature wine. [I chose MCIII for the Chairman's Trophy because it is uniquely outstanding and there is no Best in Class category for it. If any Champagne deserves a special honour, this is it, yet it might have been such a different story. When MCIII was launched earlier this year, I must confess that it was one of the few occasions when I have attended a tasting knowing I was doing so with a certain prejudice. I have seen the greatest names come unstuck and witnessed some of the most underperforming producers deliver a one-off spectacular, so I try to approach any tasting with an open mind, but one thing was bugging me about MCIII: why would Moët launch a prestige cuvée that is significantly more expensive than Dom Pérignon? Was Moët not worried that it could devalue and marginalise the most famous Champagne in history? If they had visibly spun-off DP as a distinctly separate entity, with its own purpose-built winery and no mention of Moët on the label, a minuscule production of an outlandishly priced new prestige cuvée would have been the best move it could make, as it would endow the Moët name with a Champagne of the very highest quality without anything like the volume required to challenge DP in the marketplace. But with DP commercially part of the Moët range and visibly linked to the Moët name on the label, won't MCIII simply end up fighting DP for the reputation of Moët's most prestigious Champagne? This was still spinning around in my mind as I raised my first glass to my nose, then all such extraneous thoughts flew out of my head and as soon as I tasted it, I couldn't give a damn. I was bowled over, utterly convinced and totally seduced. MCIII is one of the greatest and most intriguing Champagnes I have ever tasted. Let Moët worry about conflicting levels of prestige, I am just happy they have made this very special wine and that I have had the opportunity to taste it. And I am as pleased as punch that Moët entered it into the CSWWC 2016 and that my fellow judges agreed just how special it is, even if we had no Best in Class category to anoint it with other than, of course, the Chairman's Trophy. MCIII is a synthesis of seven true vintages and an amalgamation of three storage environments: stainless-steel, oak and glass (the III in MCIII represents the trinity of these three universes, as well as alluding the third millennium). The base wine (37-40%) was an intense, well-structured 2003, which was fermented and aged in stainless-steel vats. Added to this were the base wines of Grand Vintage 2002, 2000 and 1998 (37-40%), which were partially aged in large oak foudres and then preserved in stainless steel vats. Finally, Moët dipped into the deepest

recesses of its cellars for bottles of Grand Vintage Collection 1999, 1998 and 1993 (20-26%) to represent the universe of glass-aged wine, and emptied their contents into the mix. This MCIII assemblage was then rebottled to undergo a second fermentation (or third in the case of the Grand Vintage Collection wines). Evidently it was a bit more complicated than refermenting a few mature vintages, as the first attempt in 1998 failed. It seemed fine at first, but the fruit quickly fell over. Even Moët with its unique experience of Esprit du Siècle (11 vintages spanning every decade of the 20th century) did not get MCIII right first time. In fact MCIII 001.14 (which decodes as the first release, disgorged in 2014) was the third attempt.]

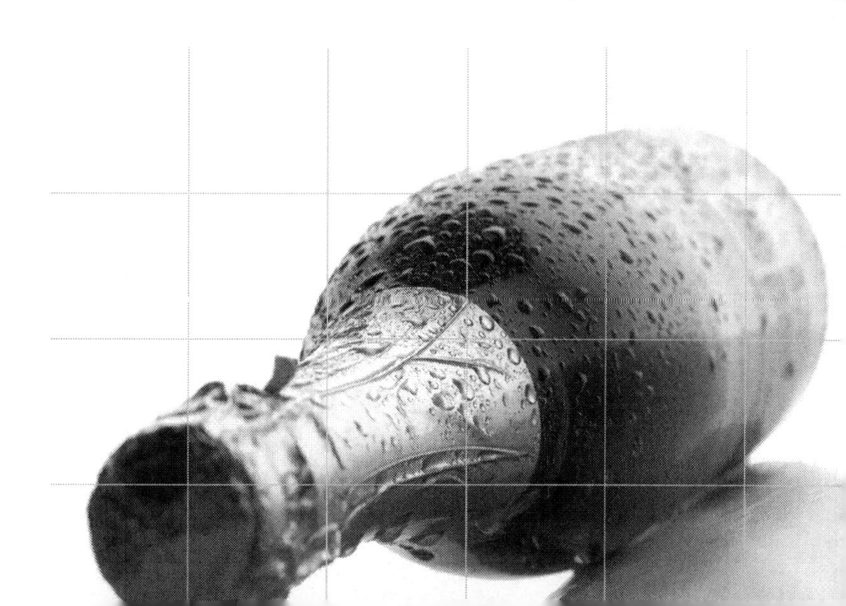

SPARKLING WINE PRODUCER OF THE YEAR

The lead-time for sparkling wine is such that as winemakers move around, they can be in a new position for 3-5 years before their own wines are released. Year after year winemakers at award-winning wineries are called to the stage to pick up awards for wines that their predecessors made and sometimes, ironically, they have might have moved on before their own wines start to collect prizes. Consequently the "Sparkling Wine Producer of the Year" recognises wineries rather than winemakers. The winner is not subject to any form of voting, but is unarguably and demonstrably the most successful producer in the competition.

I was very careful in the words I used for special award because the lead-time for a sparkling wine is such that the current winemaker is not always the person who made the wines deserving the honour, thus in the CSWWC it is "Sparkling Wine *Producer* of the Year Trophy" rather than "Sparkling *Winemaker* of the Year Award", which is the norm in other competitions. Furthermore, the winner is not subject to any form of voting, but is unarguably and demonstrably the most successful wine producer in the competition.

Champagne Louis Roederer

When Ferrari entered nine wines last year, winning an astonishing nine Gold medals, I was so amazed that I promised to eat my hat if such a feat is ever repeated. I had never witnessed so many Gold medals won by a single producer, not just at the CSWWC, but when Roederer entered 10 wines and won 10 Gold medals this year, I began tenderising my hat! Sure, the CSWWC judges all love the Roederer style, but we have never given Roederer a clean sweep of Golds before, let alone a clean sweep of 10 Golds!

The house of Louis Roederer is run today by Frédéric Rouzaud. His father Jean-Claude Rouzaud, now retired, was the cleverest and the most financially tight-fisted head of a Champagne house I have ever met. Thanks to his aversion to borrowing from the bank, he gave his son the most cash-rich, highly profitable platform in Champagne to build on. While other family-owned Champagne houses have had to hand over the day-to-day control of their businesses to professional managers from outside the family to compete in the cut and thrust of 21st century commerce, Louis Roederer has gone from strength to strength under Frédéric Rouzaud. Something that no doubt pleases his father. Frédéric's greatest assets has been his working partnership with Jean-Baptiste Lecaillon, who is not just in charge of the vineyards and winemaking, but also Deputy CEO. However tight-fisted and commercially astute a businessman is, financial success in Champagne ultimately depends on quality and style, and the reputation that generates. You can fool some customers some of the time, but you cannot fool all of them all of the time, and under Jean-Baptiste Lecaillon no one has been fooled. On his watch the quality has soared and the style honed. If pushed to articulate the style that pervades all of Louis Roederer's cuvées, from the house non-vintage to Cristal, it would be one of precision and purity, of intensity without weight and an endlessly long, tapering finish. If I had billions and could afford to cellar as much Cristal and Cristal Rosé as I like, I would still buy magnums of Brut Premier and everything between. The vintage Blanc de Blancs was once Roederer's best-kept secret, but although it is more widely known today, it remains this outstanding producer's greatest bargain.

Supreme World Champion

All the National Trophies are tasted off against each other to find the most outstanding wine in the entire competition. In 2014 it was Louis Roederer 2002 Cristal Rosé, in 2015 it was Louis Roederer 2004 Cristal Rosé, and this year it is Louis Roederer 2002 Cristal Brut in magnum.

I challenge other producers to **"Fight back!"**

For different vintages and formats of the same cuvée to rise to the top through taste-offs against a vast array of stunning sparkling wines for three consecutive years clearly indicates an extraordinary level of quality and consistency, but it is not invincible. I know a dozen producers in Champagne alone who could win this trophy. It is not as if they are not already entering stunning wines. They are. But they obviously need to target the top award and to have a chance of doing that they must first win a Best in Class and progress from there to a National Trophy. If a dozen producers go in all guns blazing with the sole aim of winning a Best in Class, it should result in several wines of a completely different styles competing for the ultimate prize.

This year's SUPREME WORLD CHAMPION

Louis Roederer 2002 Cristal Brut (Magnum)
Champagne, France (150cl, 12.50%)
55% Pinot Noir, 45% Chardonnay (10G RS%)
Absolute class, so fine and refined with an endless, creamy, tapering finish. The fruit is plush, succulent and juicy, yet its perfect balance and long, linear line provides such finesse. The fruit is so vital and seductive, supported by a mousse creams and puns in the mouth. There is a sense of grace and stature to this Champagne, and a sense of glacial evolution that knocks years off of its chronological age, this surely must be made from the finest raw materials under the guiding influence of one of today's most gifted winemakers. [Produced exclusively from Roederer's Domaine 3, which is reserved for Cristal Brut. This domaine consists of Pinot Noir in

the grands crus of Aÿ-Champagne, Beaumont-sur-Vesle, Verzenay, Verzy and a very special premier cru in Mareuil-sur-Aÿ (the lieu-dit of "les Clos", which borders the grand cru of Aÿ and many rate almost as highly), plus Chardonnay from the grands crus of Avize, Cramant and Mesnil-sur-Oger. The difference with 2002 compared to previous Cristal vintages is the increase in oak-fermented components. In the 1990s oak-fermented wines represented just 10-15 per cent of the final Cristal blend, but the oak is large foudres, the effects of which when combined with the battonage on gros lies are always textural, never aromatic.]

An A-Z of the Best Fizz

This is where to find the best fizz on the planet, all 149 Gold & 143 Silver medal wines freshly tasted and judged for this edition. No Bronze medal mediocrity here and certainly no so-called Commended wines. With these uniquely high standards, you can be certain that the winning wines of this competition are truly special. Our only *caveat* is that readers must understand that when we give a Gold or Silver medal to a magnum, we mean a magnum and a magnum only. That magnum will be different from the same wine in a 75cl bottle (*see* THE MAGNUM EFFECT EXPLAINED page 32), thus you could be disappointed if you purchase bottles. The occasional use of straight [brackets] indicates editorial comment made after the identity of the wine in question had been revealed.

PRICE GUIDE

Each wine has a price guide either supplied by the producer or based on WineSearcher Professional and correct at the time of going to press. Although the pound is worth more (barely!) than the US dollar and Euro, UK customers do not necessarily get more for their pound than other countries do for their currency, whether because of the UK's very high rate of duty or simply because the country is not known as Rip-Off Britain for nothing. Furthermore, this is an international guide and can therefore offer only an approximate price guide. That is why the three different currencies are lumped together in the key below.

$ = up to £10 / up to USD10 / up to €10
$$ = £10-20 / USD10-20 / €10-20
$$$ = £20-50 / USD20-50 / €20-50
$$$$ = £50-£100 / USD50-100 / €50-100
$$$$$ = £100+ / USD100+ / €100+

Note: Magnums are price-coded at magnum prices, thus look more expensive than the same wines in 75cl bottles, but are, of course, relatively similar (although magnums do attract a small, well-deserved premium, of course).

1+1=3

GOLD

1+1=3 2014 Brut Rosé
Cava DO, Alt Penedès, Spain (75cl, 11.50%)
80% Grenache, 15% Pinot Noir, 5% Trepat (0.7g RS)

- Best Cava Rosé
- Best Cava
- Best Spanish Sparkling Wine

When critics discuss red and white wines, you may hear mention of "the New Spain". Well, this is "the New Cava" and, specifically "the New Cava Rosado": delicate in colour, fruit and weight. So light, long and fine, fresh, youthful peachy fruit and long, soft, linear finish. Crisp and zesty, with a lovely freshness and easiness to it. **$ per bottle**

ADAMI

SILVER

Col Credas Rive di Farra di Soligo 2015 Brut
Valdobbiadene Prosecco Superiore DOCG (Rive), Veneto, Italy (75cl, 11%)
100% Glera (4g RS)
Fresh aromatics followed by soft, succulent, juicy-fresh, peachy fruit. Despite a finish that is quite abrupt, this is a well-deserved Silver. With another 2-3 grams of residual sugar, it might well be Gold medal quality. **$$ per bottle**

AKARUA

GOLD

Akarua Rosé NV Methode Traditionelle
Bannockburn, Central Otago, New Zealand (75cl, 13%)
52% Chardonnay, 48% Pinot Noir (4.7g RS)
Very pretty, pale-peach colour with fresh, youthful, fruit-driven aromas followed by serious, Chardonnay-dominated, yeast-complexed fruit on a crisp, succulent palate. Lengthy with a refreshing brut finish. **$$ per bottle**

SILVER

Akarua Vintage 2010 Methode Traditionelle
Bannockburn, Central Otago, New Zealand (75cl, 13%)
54% Pinot Noir, 46% Chardonnay (6.1g RS)
Pale-lemon green colour with a soft, creamy-leesy aroma and a round, fleshy palate of bright fruit. Rather singular but succulent. **$$$ per bottle**

SILVER

Akarua Vintage 2011 Methode Traditionelle
Bannockburn, Central Otago, New Zealand (75cl, 13%)
60% Pinot Noir, 40% Chardonnay (6g RS)
Pale-lemon-green, fine aroma, touch of complexity. All freshness and vitality on the palate, which caries to a nice, crisp, brut finish. **$$$ per bottle**

ANDREOLA

SILVER

ANDREOLA 2015 MILLESIMATO
Valdobbiadene Prosecco Superiore DOCG, Veneto, Italy (75cl, 11%)
100% Glera (24g RS)
Fresh, grassy aromatics with soft, spicy notes. Very fresh and feisty, not too sweet. Lovely creamy mousse. **$$ per bottle**

ANTICA FRATTA

GOLD

ANTICA FRATTA 2011 ESSENCE ROSÉ
Franciacorta DOCG, Lombardy, Italy (75cl, 13%)
55% Pinot Noir, 45% Chardonnay (6.5g RS)
Starbright very pale salmon colour, with nicely restrained, refined gunpowder and toast aromas. Long and zesty, gliding to a fine, fresh, dry finish. **$$$ per bottle**

SILVER

ANTICA FRATTA NV BRUT
Franciacorta DOCG, Lombardy, Italy (75cl, 13%)
90% Chardonnay, 10% Pinot Noir (6.5g RS)
Ripe floral-Chardonnay aroma, with freshness and vitality on the palate. Crisp and fluffy. **$$ per bottle**

ASTORIA

SILVER

ASTORIA 2015 EXTRA-DRY
Valdobbiadene Prosecco Superiore DOCG, Veneto, Italy (75cl, 11.50%)
100% Glera (17g RS)
Lovely, super-fresh, super-fragrant fruit with a hint of spice and a super-smooth mousse. Soft white fruit aromas. Crisp, easy and friendly. **$$ per bottle**

AZAHARA

SILVER

AZAHARA NV MOSCATO
Murray Darling, Victoria, Australia (75cl, 6%)
100% Moscato (100g RS)
Pale-lemon colour with green flecks and a lovely, fresh, lime-influenced Moscato aroma, which follows quickly onto the palate. Soft mousse and a good acid balance. The finishes is rich, creamy and sweet with notes of raisins, orange blossom on the aftertaste. **$$ per bottle**

BARNAUT

GOLD

Barnaut Authentique NV Grand Cru Rosé
Champagne, France (75cl, 12.50%)
85% Pinot Noir, 15% Chardonnay (6g RS)

- Best Champagne NV Rosé
- Best Grower Champagne

A classic Champagne with a lovely Pinot presence. Complex red-fruit aromatics with light, developed notes of spiced-toast and pencil shavings. Rich, almost sweet impression of crisp fruit on a smooth palate with a lovely, velvety-dry finish. **$$$ per bottle**

BEAUMONT DES CRAYÈRES

SILVER

Beaumont des Crayères NV Grande Réserve
Champagne, France (75cl, 12.40%)
60% Meunier, 25% Chardonnay, 15% Pinot Noir (5.9g RS)
A fresh and singular Champagne of easy appeal. Apricot aroma leads to a crisp and deliciously fruity palate with a certain creaminess and a well-judged dosage for mass-appeal.. **$$$ per bottle**

BELLAVEDER

SILVER

Bellaveder 2011 Brut Nature Riserva
Trentodoc, Trentino Alto Adige, Italy (75cl, 13%)
100% Chardonnay (1.8g RS)
White fruit aroma with vanilla-laden toasted and honeyed notes. Rich fruit, impressive. Sunshine in a bottle! **$$$ per bottle**

GOLD

Bellaveder 2011 Brut Riserva
Trentodoc, Trentino Alto Adige, Italy (75cl, 13%)
100% Chardonnay (6.4g RS)
Restrained gunpowdery aromas with pineapple-dominated tropical fruit and a lean, beautifully-focused palate structure. Light in weight, with lovely emerging toast aromas and hints of oak complexity. **$$$ per bottle**

BESSERAT DE BELLEFON

GOLD

Besserat de Bellefon Cuvée des Moines NV Blanc de Blancs Grand Cru
Champagne, France (75cl, 12.50%)
100% Chardonnay (8.5g RS)
Soft, restrained mellow aromas with refined toasty notes. Lovely fluffy creamy palate with lemony fruit and classic linear structure. Highly pleasurable. **$$$ per bottle**

BIONDELLI

GOLD

BIONDELLI NV BRUT (MAGNUM)
Franciacorta DOCG, Lombardy, Italy (150cl, 12.50%)
100% Chardonnay (6g RS)

- Best Franciacorta NV Blanc de Blancs
- Best Value Franciacorta

Stylish, super-fresh acacia aromas, with notes of ripe yellow apples, yellow plums and toast. Crisp fluffy palate, a sumptuous mousse, and a long, focused finish beautifully balanced by fruit-acidity. **$$ per magnum**

BISOL VITIVINICOLTORI

GOLD

BISOL 2015 CARTIZZE
Prosecco Superiore di Valdobbiadene di Cartizze DOCG, Veneto, Italy (75cl, 11.40%)
100% Glera (24g RS)
Lovely light-spicy aromatics introduce a fresh, firm and zesty palate where the fruit is not too sweet. **$$$ per bottle**

BODEGAS BILBAÍNAS

SILVER

VIÑA POMAL 2013 BLANC DE NOIRS GARNACHA RESERVA
Cava DO, Rioja, Spain (75cl, 12%)
100% Garnacha Tinta (10.5g RS)
Pale-lemon colour with a peachy hue. Attractive, rosé-like, red-fruit aroma. Lovely fruit, freshness and crisp structure. **$$ per bottle**

BOHIGAS

SILVER

BOHIGAS NV BRUT NATURE RESERVA
Cava DO, Barcelona, Spain (75cl, 12%)
50% Xarel-lo, 30% Macabeo, 20% Parellada (1.6g RS)
Lovely, bright, pale lemon-green colour. Fresh and elegant, red and white fruit aromas with a few nicely spiced notes. A crisp, dry and refreshing palate of bright, clean fruitiness over a super-fluffy mousse. **$$ per bottle**

BOLNEY WINE ESATE

SILVER

BOLNEY 2013 CUVÉE ROSÉ
Sussex, England (75cl, 12.50%)
100% Pinot Noir (6g RS)
Mid-peach colour. Lovely toast overlaying Pinot fruitiness on a stylishly creamy palate with fine acid line. **$$$ per bottle**

BOUVET LADUBAY

GOLD

BOUVET SAUMUR SAPHIR 2013 BRUT
Saumur AOC, Loire, France (75cl, 12%)
80% Chenin Blanc, 20% Chardonnay (11g RS)

- Best Loire Blend
- Best Loire Sparkling Wine

Pale-lemon colour. Soft lemon and yellow-apple aromas. Crisp palate and fluffy mousse. Fresh, elegant, rather delicate style of developed Chenin fruit. **$ per bottle**

GOLD

BOUVET SAUMUR TRESOR 2012 BRUT
Saumur AOC, Loire, France (75cl, 12%)
60% Chenin Blanc, 40% Chardonnay (12g RS)
Refined, yeast-complexed aromas with enticing notes of ripe apples lying in straw. Fresh and vivacious, with a nice acid line. Youthful despite the evolved character. Good length and a creamy brut balance. **$ per bottle**

CAMEL VALLEY

GOLD

CAMEL VALLEY 2013 PINOT NOIR BRUT (PINK LABEL)
England (75cl, 12.50%)
100% Pinot Noir (11g RS)
Mid-salmon. Stylishly red-fruit nose with exuberant Pinot fruit on a silky palate. Long, zingy and focused, tapering to t lovely dry finish. A masterpiece of youthful Pinot elegance. **$$$ per bottle**

SILVER

CAMEL VALLEY 2014 CHARDONNAY BRUT
England (75cl, 12.50%)
100% Chardonnay (11g RS)
Very pale colour. Lovely, fresh, vibrant fruit on a creamy palate, with a long, tangy and tapered finish. Great acids. Should gradually go toasty. I would like to keep this a year before broaching the first bottles. **$$$ per bottle**

CANARD-DUCHÊNE

SILVER

CANARD-DUCHÊNE AUTHENTIC VINTAGE 2008 BRUT
Champagne, France (75cl, 12%)
30% Chardonnay, 40% Pinot Noir, 30% Meunier (11.1g RS)
Developing aromas with some earthy-spicy complexity and under-control oxidative notes. Juicy succulent palate, linear and energetic, with very crisp, yeast-complexed fruit with a long, creamy finish. **$$$ per bottle**

GOLD

CANARD-DUCHÊNE LA GRANDE CUVÉE CHARLES VII NV BLANC DE NOIRS
Champagne, France (75cl, 12%)
70% Pinot Noir, 30% Meunier (11g RS)
Lovely toast-complexed Pinot aromas on nose and palate. Soft and mellow, with lovely vanilla-dusted fruit. A highly pleasurable Champagne with the structure and drive to improve in bottle. **$$$ per bottle**

CANTINA D'ISERA

GOLD

CANTINA D'ISERA NV EXTRA BRUT
Trentodoc, Trentino Alto Adige, Italy (75cl, 12.50%)
100% Chardonnay (3g RS)
Attractively toasty nose with a firm, fresh and ripe fruit profile. Creamy and satisfying on the palate. Long and linear with a good brut finish. **$$ per bottle**

CANTINA ROTALIANA DI MEZZOLOMBARDO

SILVER

CANTINA ROTALIANA DI MEZZOLOMBARDO NV REDOR
Trentodoc, Trentino Alto Adige, Italy (75cl, 12.50%)
100% Chardonnay, None (8.7g RS)
Mellow, floral-vanilla aroma with a few toasty notes beginning to emerge. Very young, fresh, zippy fruit on a crisp palate with lovely, satiny, brut finish. **$ per bottle**

CARACCIOLI CELLARS

GOLD

CARACCIOLI CELLARS 2007 BRUT CUVÉE (MAGNUM)
Santa Lucia Highlands AVA, California, USA (150cl, 12%)
40% Pinot Noir, 60% Chardonnay (12g RS)
Pale-lemon colour. Delicate, soft , creamy-pure fruity aromas with notes of vanilla and white fruit. Lovely toast, charred oak and super zingy acidity. **$$$ per magnum**

GOLD

CARACCIOLI CELLARS 2007 BRUT ROSÉ (MAGNUM)
Santa Lucia Highlands AVA, California, USA (150cl, 12%)
40% Pinot Noir, 60% Chardonnay (11.5g RS)
Beautiful, pale pink-peach colour. Gorgeous toasty nose, plush Pinot fruit. Super high, crisp acids. Stylish, yet could be even better with more time on yeast. **$$$$ per magnum**

SILVER

Caracciolí Cellars 2010 Brut Cuvée (Magnum)
Santa Lucia Highlands AVA, California, USA (75cl, 12.10%)
40% Pinot Noir, 60% Chardonnay (12g RS)
Pale colour with a peachy hue. Gently yeast-complexed, peach-fruit aroma with crisp and zingy, bright fruit on the palate. Lovely balance of fruit and high acidity with very slick and sophisticated barrel-ferment notes. Great elegance and finesse. **$$$ per bottle**

SILVER

Caracciolí Cellars 2010 Brut Rosé
Santa Lucia Highlands AVA, California, USA (75cl, 11.70%)
40% Pinot Noir, 60% Chardonnay (11.5g RS)
Bright cherry-pink colour. High-class barrel fermentation aromas are evolving into sumptuous, toast and red-fruit notes with spicy-vanilla complexity, with a soft, cushiony mousse carrying gorgeous fruit to a very crisp brut finish. **$$$$ per bottle**

CASTELLBLANCH

SILVER

Castellblanch Zero 2011 Brut Reserva
Cava DO, Spain (75cl, 11.30%)
30% Macabeo, 60% Parellada, 10% Xarel-lo (7g RS)
Pale-lemon colour, with traditional terpene-infused Cava aroma followed by rich, crisp, sweet and zesty fruit. This wine has a long and linear, fine dry finish. Excellent acidity. **$$ per bottle**

CASTELLO BONOMI

SILVER

Castello Bonomi NV Cruperdù (Magnum)
Franciacorta DOCG, Lombardy, Italy (150cl, 12.50%)
70% Chardonnay, 30% Pinot Noir (5.3g RS)
Attractively developed aromatics with notes of mild vanilla toast follow on to a crisp palate of yeast-complexed fruit and a lovely creamy mousse. **$$$ per magnum**

CASTLE BROOK

GOLD

Castle Brook 2010 Classic Cuvée
Herefordshire, England (75cl, 12%)
51% Chardonnay, 30% Pinot Noir, 19% Meunier (7g RS)
Soft, easy and gentle with super-stylish, spiced-toast aromas and lovely crisp fruit on the palate. **$$$ per bottle**

CEMBRA CANTINA DI MONTAGNA

SILVER

Cembra Cantina di Montagna NV Ororosso Dosaggio Zero
Trentodoc, Trentino Alto Adige, Italy (75cl, 12.50%)
100% Chardonnay (2.7g RS)
Mid-lemon colour. Fruity, yeast-complexed aroma with light toasty notes. Such a full, round and intense palate that there is an almost liquorice concentration of fruit, fresh brut finish. **$$ per bottle**

CESARINI SFORZA

SILVER

Cesarini Sforza Tridentvm Riserva 2008 Brut
Trentodoc, Trentino Alto Adige, Italy (75cl, 12.50%)
100% Chardonnay (3.8g RS)
Light on aromatics, but with a touch of complexity. Plenty of enjoyable and satisfying fruit on the palate. Very dry, but very well balanced, with lovely, fluffy mousse a dry brut finish. **$$$ per bottle**

CHANDON AUSTRALIA

GOLD

Chandon 2005 Prestige Cuvée
Yarra Valley, Australia (75cl, 13.20%)
56% Chardonnay, 36% Pinot Noir, 8% Meunier (5g RS)

- Best Australian Vintaged Blend
- Best Australian Sparkling Wine

The pedigree of this wine was obvious to at least one of the judges, who wrote "Classic Moët gunpowder: is this a Chandon?" Superbly toasty, beautiful charred and exuberantly fruity nose. Voluptuous, round and succulent, with a soft, long and lovely, creamy finish. **$$$ per bottle**

GOLD

Chandon 2012 Blanc de Blancs
Yarra Valley, Australia (75cl, 12.70%)
100% Chardonnay (5g RS)
Mid-lemon in colour with a fresh with white-fruit aromas This is an elegant and highly polished style of blanc de blancs with yeast-complexed fruits on the palate, tapering to a very fresh, fine brut finish. **$$$ per bottle**

GOLD

Chandon 2012 Vintage Brut
Yarra Valley, Australia (75cl, 12.30%)
51% Pinot Noir, 45% Chardonnay, 4% Meunier (5g RS)
Pale-lemon colour with beautifully light and lingering, ethereal aromas of brioche and light-toast mingling with bright yet delicate notes of white-fruit. This wine has lovely, fresh, fine-tuned and highly polished fruit on the palate, with an invigoratingly firm brut finish. **$$$ per bottle**

SILVER

CHANDON 2012 VINTAGE COLLECTION CUVÉE

Yarra Valley, Australia (75cl, 12.50%)
70% Chardonnay, 29% Pinot Noir, 1% Meunier (5g RS)
Mid-lemon colour. Beautiful, toast-laden, Chardonnay driven aroma. Very little yeast-aged complexity, but the palate has plenty of fruit, a deep, rich and powerful flavour, and tapers nicely to a dry brut finish. Would be even better with another year on yeast, which is a compliment. **$$$ per bottle**

CHANDON CHINA

SILVER

CHANDON NV BRUT

Helan Mountain's East Foothills, Ningxia, China (75cl, 12.50%)
70% Chardonnay, 30% Pinot Noir (9g RS)
Mid-lemon colour. Soft and mellow aromas, clean, with ripe fruitiness and leesy complexity. Super soft palate with creamy mousse and sufficient length thanks to a finely balanced dosage. **$$ per bottle**

GOLD

CHANDON NV BRUT ROSÉ

Helan Mountain's East Foothills, Ningxia, China (75cl, 12.50%)
70% Chardonnay, 30% Pinot Noir (9g RS)

- Best Chinese Rosé
- Best Chinese Sparkling Wine

A medium-cherry pink colour followed by a stylishly fragrant nose of red cherry vibrancy with attractive toasty notes. Firm, with a soft, spicy palate and a long, well-balanced, true Brut finish. This is not only the best Chinese sparkling wine we have tasted, it is the best Asian sparkling wine by some distance [despite the youthfulness of the operation]. **$$ per bottle**

CHAPEL DOWN

GOLD

CHAPEL DOWN 2010 THREE GRACES

Kent, England (75cl, 12%)
60% Chardonnay, 33% Pinot Noir, 7% Meunier (9g RS)
Toasty-leesy aromas highlighted by distinctive notes of pastry richness. This is a firm, vibrant, intensely fruity, with pineapple-flavoured fruit-acidity dominating before tapering to a nicely dry finish. **$$$ per bottle**

SILVER

CHAPEL DOWN NV VINTAGE RESERVE ROSÉ

Kent, England (75cl, 12%)
100% Pinot Noir (10.5g RS)
Pale salmon-peach colour. Stylish Pinot aroma with some aged complexity. Fresh, crisp, balanced and friendly, with good weight, carry and balance.
$$$ per bottle

CHARLES HEIDSIECK

GOLD

Charles Heidsieck 1989 Brut Jeroboam
Champagne, France (300cl, 12%)
55% Pinot Noir, 45% Chardonnay (12.2g RS)
- Best Champagne Library Vintage

Beautiful freshly-disgorged aromatics with notes of spiced toast, rich honey, roast coffee, vanilla and fudge. Concentrated fruit. Velvety. A long finish, leaving an aftertaste that is more wine than Champagne. Compelling stuff.
$$$$$ per jeroboam

GOLD

Charles Heidsieck 2006 Rosé Millésime
Champagne, France (75cl, 12.50%)
60% Pinot Noir, 40% Chardonnay (11.4g RS)
A full, creamy-toasty aroma, followed by plush ripe fruitiness on a long, smooth and very clean palate, with a lovely finish. **$$$$ per bottle**

GOLD

Charles Heidsieck NV Brut Réserve
Champagne, France (75cl, 12.80%)
33% Pinot Noir, 34% Meunier, 33% Chardonnay (11.2g RS)
- Best Champagne NV Blend
- World Champion Classic NV Brut Blend

This wonderfully toasty Champagne is more like a cellar-aged non-vintage than the current non-vintage blend. Lovely, roasted-coffee aromas with notes of honey and dried-fruit. Calm, concentrated and long. **$$$ per bottle**

GOLD

Charles Heidsieck NV Rosé Réserve
Champagne, France (75cl, 12.40%)
33% Pinot Noir, 34% Meunier, 33% Chardonnay (11.2g RS)
Starbright, pale-salmon colour, this is a very classy and serious rosé with lovely, layered aromas of peachy fruit with slow-evolving notes of vanilla and coffee notes, leading to smooth and caressing palate of spiced-fruit. A Champagne of great vivacity and a long, lingering, soft and mellow finish.
$$$$ per bottle

CHATEAU TANUNDA

SILVER

Chateau Tanunda 2012 Blanc de Blancs Brut
Eden Valley, South Australia, Australia (75cl, 12.50%)
100% Chardonnay (9.4g RS)
Pale-lemon colour. Quite refined nose, with plenty of ripe fruit. Rich, weighty and serious on the palate, which has a crisp brut finish. Not typically blanc de blancs in style, even for a weightier version, but very enjoyable in its own way. **$$ per bottle**

CLOVER HILL

SILVER

Clover Hill 2012 Brut
Tasmania, Australia (75cl, 12%)
65% Chardonnay, 30% Pinot Noir, 4% Meunier, 1% Pinot Gris (7.5g RS)
Mid-lemon colour, with a ripe fruit profile and notes of toast, liquorice and tropical fruits. An overt, round and fleshy palate, yet lighter in body than the depth of its fruit might suggest. Crisp brut finish. **$$ per bottle**

COATES & SEELY

SILVER

Coates & Seely 2009 La Perfide Blanc de Blancs
Hampshire, England (75cl, 12%)
100% Chardonnay (7.3g RS)
Lovely yeast-complexed fruit aroma with pastry notes. Super-acidic palate, long and lean with a balance on the dry side. **$$$ per bottle**

GOLD

Coates & Seely NV Brut Réserve
Hampshire, England (75cl, 12%)
65% Chardonnay, 17% Pinot Noir, 18% Meunier (10g RS)
Stylish, well-integrated and nuanced zesty aromas that lead on to a creamy palate teeming with tangy fruit long and linear finish. **$$$ per bottle**

CODORNIU

SILVER

Anna de Codorníu NV Blanc de Blancs Brut Reserva (Magnum)
Cava DO, Catalunya, Spain (150cl, 11.90%)
70% Chardonnay, 15% Parellada, 8% Macabeo, 7% Xarel-lo (10.5g RS)
Mid-lemon colour. Soft, easy-drinking, gorgeous fruit and a sumptuous mousse: what more do you want? A very classy Silver. **$$$ per magnum**

SILVER

Anna de Codorníu NV Brut (Magnum)
Cava DO, Catalunya, Spain (150cl, 11.50%)
70% Chardonnay, 15% Parellada, 8% Xarel-lo, 7% Macabeo (7.5g RS)
Mid-lemon colour. Freshness overlaying spicy aromas of traditional Cava typicity. Gorgeous mousse, lovely, luscious fruit, with a sweet brut finish and good mouthfeel. Very elegant, very long. Pristine. **$$$ per magnum**

SILVER

Codorníu Non Plus Ultra NV Brut Reserva
Cava DO, Catalunya, Spain (75cl, 11.50%)
50% Parellada, 40% Macabeo, 10% Xarel-lo (8g RS)
Mid-lemon colour. Evolving nose of spice and charred characters. Ripe fruit profile. Rich and tasty with a very creamy finish. **$$ per bottle**

GOLD

Gran Codorníu Gran Reserva Pinot Noir 2009 Finca El Coster
Cava DO, Catalunya, Spain (75cl, 12%)
100% Pinot Noir (11g RS)
Evolving, spicy-earthy Pinot aromas lead to rich and tasty Pinot fruit on a firm and zesty palate, which boasts an exceptionally linear structure with truly lovely acids for a Cava. This is a classy wine by any standards. **$$$ per bottle**

SILVER

Gran Codorníu Gran Reserva Pinot Noir 2009 Finca El Coster
Cava DO, Spain (75cl, 12%)
100% Pinot Noir (12g RS)
Mid-lemon colour. Soft and round vanilla aroma over peach and yellow fruits. Pure Pinot fruit on the palate, which has a classic structure, great acid-line and yeast complexed notes on aftertaste. [A different disgorgement date than the Gold medal winner, and one gram extra of dosage.] **$$$ per bottle**

SILVER

Gran Codorníu Pinot Noir 2013 Vintage Brut
Cava DO, Catalunya, Spain (75cl, 12.30%)
100% Pinot Noir (11.5g RS)
Cherry colour. Sweet Pinot fruit, with strawberry from riper fruit and red cherry from the Pinot picked for acidity. Crisp, clean and full of fruit. **$$ per bottle**

COLLALTO

SILVER

Collalto 2015 Rosé Extra Dry
Incrocio Manzoni Moscato Marca Trevigiana IGP, Veneto, Italy (75cl, 11.50%)
100% Incrocio Manzoni Moscato (17g RS)
Beautifully pale pink-peach colour. Sweet peardrop fruit aromas with hint of Moscato and fragrant, candied strawberry notes, followed by a sweet Muscat palate caressed by a cushiony soft mousse. **$$ per bottle**

COLLET

GOLD

Collet NV Extra Brut
Champagne, France (75cl, 12.50%)
40% Chardonnay, 40% Pinot Noir, 20% Meunier (3g RS)
Stylish layered nose with nice vanilla and toasty notes, a soft, mellow palate with creamy mousse and fresh balanced finish. This Champagne takes its low dosage extremely well. **$$$ per bottle**

COTTONWORTH

GOLD

COTTONWORTH NV CLASSIC CUVÉE
Hampshire, England (75cl, 12%)
60% Chardonnay, 27% Pinot Noir, 13% Meunier (7.9g RS)
Stylish nose, well balanced and well built, this is a classy English sparkling wine with a classically lean structure and fresh, zingy, succulent fruit. **$$$ per bottle**

GOLD

COTTONWORTH NV SPARKLING ROSÉ
Hampshire, England (75cl, 12%)
43% Meunier, 32% Pinot Noir, 18% Chardonnay, 7% Pinot Noir Précoce (12.8g RS)
A pale-apricot colour, with youthful, peach-fruit aroma and a crisp, zesty palate teeming with elegant cool fruit. Very fruity, but has the structure, balance and length to take it. **$$$ per bottle**

CRICOVA

SILVER

CRICOVA NV ROZ BRUT
Moldova (75cl, 12.30%)
90% Pinot Noir, 10% Cabernet Sauvignon (6g RS)
Delicate, pale-pink colour. Lovely crisp red fruits on the nose, with a clean, crisp, bright-fruit palate. Not complex, but nicely polished and long. **$ per bottle**

CUVAGE

SILVER

CUVAGE NV ROSÉ
Nebbiolo d'Alba DOC, Piemonte, Italy (75cl, 12%)
100% Nebbiolo (12g RS)
Very pretty pale-salmon colour. A fruity palate with cardamom, red berries and a lovely acid-line for a long, succulent finish. [Last year's Chairman's Trophy now has a precise DOC and next year it will carry a vintage.] **$$$ per bottle**

DE CASTELNAU

SILVER

DE CASTELNAU NV BRUT ROSÉ
Champagne, France (75cl, 12.50%)
51% Meunier, 35% Chardonnay, 14% Pinot Noir (10g RS)
Bright bronze-pink colour with orange hues. Mature, peach-fruit aroma. Not a complex Champagne, but has lovely juicy fruit on the palate and a succulent, fairly long finish. **$$$ per bottle**

SILVER
De Castelnau NV Cuvée Hors Categorie
Champagne, France (75cl, 12.50%)
55% Pinot Noir, 28% Meunier, 17% Chardonnay (6g RS)
Overt, ripe fruit aroma with notes of tropical fruit and vanilla. A broad, tasty, rich palate with a calm mousse and a fine lingering, soft brut finish.
$$$ per bottle

DE SAINT GALL

GOLD
De Saint Gall 2002 Millésime
Champagne, France (75cl, 12.50%)
100% Chardonnay (7g RS)
Classy toast-laden aroma with perfumed notes and gunpowdery hues. Not so much classic Champagne as classic 2002, the super-ripe and generous fruitiness of the aromatic are heading towards dried fruits, with a wide, winey, almost oily-rich palate that is caressingly soft and vinous, yet still possesses a great acid line, leading to a beautiful and surprisingly linear finish. **$$$ per bottle**

SILVER
De Saint Gall NV Extra Brut
Champagne, France (75cl, 12.50%)
100% Chardonnay (5g RS)
Beautiful, toast-laden aroma with complex notes of caramel, vanilla and crème brulée. Creamy and caressing on the palate, which has a classic lean structure and brimming with beautifully fresh and classy, toasted Chardonnay fruit. **$$ per bottle**

DENBIES WINE ESTATE

SILVER
Denbies Greenfields NV Brut
Surrey, England (75cl, 12%)
52% Pinot Noir, 48% Chardonnay (9.3g RS)
Attractive and refined nose with a toastiness to it. The palate is soft in texture, with a mellowness, yet crisp with acidity and a dry brut finish. **$$$ per bottle**

DEUTZ

GOLD
Amour de Deutz 2006 Brut
Champagne, France (75cl, 12.10%)
100% Chardonnay (8.5g RS)
Stylish and harmonious, yeast-complexed, fruity aroma with complexing notes of baking spice. Fresh, seamless and elegant. Classy fruit. Fresh, light and elegant. Long and vibrant. **$$$$$ per bottle**

SILVER
DEUTZ NV BRUT ROSÉ
Champagne, France (75cl, 12.20%)
90% Pinot Noir, 10% Chardonnay (10.5g RS)
Pale-salmon colour with delicate and fragrant aromas. Lovely, young, fresh, vibrantly fruity style. **$$$ per bottle**

GOLD
WILLIAM DEUTZ 2006 BRUT
Champagne, France (75cl, 12.20%)
66% Pinot Noir, 29% Chardonnay, 5% Meunier (8.8g RS)
Soft and appealing yeast-complexed fruit aromas enriched with pastry nuances and bright, very ripe fruit a fresh palate. **$$$$ per bottle**

DEVAUX

GOLD
DEVAUX CUVÉE D NV AGED 5 YEARS (MAGNUM)
Champagne, France (150cl, 12%)
55% Pinot Noir, 45% Chardonnay (9.6g RS)
Classic, stylish, yeast-complexed aromas, with toast and vanilla spiciness. Textbook lean structure and creamy, linear palate. **$$$$$ per magnum**

GOLD
DEVAUX D ROSÉ NV AGED 5 YEARS (MAGNUM)
Champagne, France (150cl, 12%)
55% Pinot Noir, 45% Chardonnay (7.3g RS)
Pale-salmon colour, with fresh, fragrant, restrained youthful aromas that will age super-gracefully. Crisp, succulent palate with delicate, easy-drinking, juicy fruit finish and creamy aftertaste. **$$$$$ per magnum**

GOLD
DEVAUX ULTRA D NV AGED 5 YEARS (MAGNUM)
Champagne, France (150cl, 12%)
55% Pinot Noir, 45% Chardonnay (4.2g RS)
- Best Low or No Dosage Champagne

Ripe red-apple aromas highlighted by spiced notes, followed by a plush, fruity palate with a nice succulence. This is a sumptuous Champagne of finesse and style that will go lovely and toasty. **$$$$$ per magnum**

DIGBY FINE ENGLISH

SILVER
DIGBY FINE ENGLISH 2010 VINTAGE BRUT
England (75cl, 12%)
60% Chardonnay, 32% Pinot Noir, 8% Meunier (8g RS)
Soft white-fruit aroma. Crisp, lemony fruit. Tart, vibrant fruit on palate. Long and very crisp. Still commendably tight and youthful. **$$$ per bottle**

DOM PÉRIGNON

GOLD

Dom Pérignon Blanc 1998 P2
Champagne, France (75cl, 12%)
55% Chardonnay, 45% Pinot Noir (5g RS)
Super-complex, mellow and honeyed aroma with notes of vanilla, gunpowder and pastry, followed by a pert and perky, youthful palate with full, yet lithe and lively, Pinot-dominated fruit. Long and focused with a linear-driven finish. **$$$$$ per bottle**

GOLD

Dom Pérignon Rosé 1995 P2
Champagne, France (75cl, 12%)
42% Chardonnay, 58% Pinot Noir (6.5g RS)

- Best Deluxe Champagne Library Vintage
- World Champion Library Vintage

Deep copper colour with bronzed highlights. Absolutely beautiful Pinot aromas, with mellow, spiced-cherry complexity and notes of chocolate and forest-floor. Great exuberance of fruit on the palate. Positively vinous, with an intense, vibrant and lingering richness. Firm , muscular and full of life for 20-plus years of age, yet velvet-textured, with great focus and freshness, with a lovely, satisfying brut finish. **$$$$$ per bottle**

DOMAINE DES DIEUX

GOLD

Domaine des Dieux 2010 Claudia Brut
Cap Classique, Walker Bay, Western Cape, South Africa (75cl, 12%)
81% Chardonnay, 19% Pinot Noir, None (7.7g RS)
Mid-lemon colour, stylishly toasty, with a sweet vanilla-laden nose over glossy, ripe, white-fruits. Fresh and fluffy. **$$ per bottle**

ENDRIZZI

SILVER

Endrizzi 2009 Rosè Piancastello
Trentodoc, Trentino Alto Adige, Italy (75cl, 12.50%)
100% Pinot Noir (9g RS)
Ultra-pale Roederer-like Rosé colour, with super-refined, elegantly developed toasty aromas and seamless, lingering fruit. **$$ per bottle**

EXTON PARK WINES

SILVER

Exton Park Wines 2011 Blanc de Blanc
Hampshire, England (75cl, 11.50%), 100% Chardonnay (8.3g RS)
Very classy green-spice, tobacco-leaf and toasty-oak aroma, with exuberant, super-zingy fruit. Mouth-watering. **$$$ per bottle**

SILVER

Exton Park Wines NV Blanc de Noir
Hampshire, England (75cl, 11.50%)
100% Pinot Noir (10g RS)
Refined, pure white fruit aromas with nicely balanced, fine Pinot fruit on a crisp, tangy palate. Very youthful and tight. **$$$ per bottle**

SILVER

Exton Park Wines NV Rosé
Hampshire, England (75cl, 11.50%)
70% Pinot Noir, 30% Meunier (8.5g RS)
Gorgeously pale salmon colour. Sweet strawberry fruit. Crisp, fresh and elegant. **$$$ per bottle**

FERRARI

GOLD

Ferrari NV Brut
Trentodoc, Trentino Alto Adige, Italy (75cl, 12.50%)
100% Chardonnay (6g RS)
Lovely, mellow, vanilla and creamy-toast aromas. Also tropical fruits. Zingy, fresh palate of bright fruit. Beautifully balanced. **$$ per bottle**

GOLD

Ferrari NV Brut (Magnum)
Trentodoc, Trentino Alto Adige, Italy (150cl, 12.50%)
100% Chardonnay (6g RS)

- Best Trentodoc NV Blanc de Blancs
- Best Trentodoc Magnum
- Best Trentodoc
- Best Italian Sparkling Wine
- World Champion Classic Blanc de Blancs

Autolytic notes over ripe citrus fruit with toast building up. Intense, but not at all weighty, linear fruit, crisp, zesty and full of life. Lovely, tapering length with fine acid line. Voluminous mousse adds creaminess to the finish. Classic Blanc de Blancs. **$$$ per magnum**

GOLD

Ferrari Perlé 2008 Blanc de Blancs Brut (Magnum)
Trentodoc, Trentino Alto Adige, Italy (150cl, 12.50%)
100% Chardonnay (5g RS)

- Best Trentodoc Vintaged Blanc de Blancs

A classic and classy blanc de blanc, with deep, developed, super-toasty aromas, biscuity notes, and lovely linear palate oozing with concentrated fruit. **$$$$ per magnum**

SILVER

Ferrari Perlé Nero 2008 Blanc de Noirs
Trentodoc, Trentino Alto Adige, Italy (75cl, 12.50%)
100% Pinot Noir (3g RS)
Rapeseed aroma followed by intense barrel-fermented Pinot fruit notes, with complexing hints of toast and nuts . Very rich fruit on palate, but also very long, with a tapering finish. Which carry to palate. Strong linear palate that carries long to a brut finish. **$$$$ per bottle**

GOLD

Ferrari Riserva Lunelli 2007 Blanc de Blancs
Trentodoc, Trentino Alto Adige, Italy (75cl, 12.50%)
100% Chardonnay (3g RS)
- Best Trentodoc Low or No Dosage

A bright golden colour with elegant, slowly-evolved, toasty aromas, this wine has a lovely acidity driving the intensity of its voluptuous fruit on the palate. Long and succulent with a fine, dry, brut finish. **$$$$ per bottle**

GOLD

Giulio Ferrari Riserva del Fondatore 2000 Blanc de Blancs (Magnum)
Trentodoc, Trentino Alto Adige, Italy (150cl, 12.50%)
100% Chardonnay (5g RS)
The beautiful roasted-coffee, buttered-toast, honey and perfumed aromatics in this wine are so seductive that one judge wrote "the brain is reluctant to allow the hand to move the glass from nose to mouth to actually taste it"! The fruit on the palate is, however, well worth the wait. This is super-toasty, mature Chardonnay at its very best. Outstanding by any standard, in magnum this is one of the very greatest Italian sparkling wines ever produced. **$$$$$ per magnum**

FRANCA CONTEA

GOLD

Franca Contea 2010 Satèn Millesimato
Franciacorta DOCG, Lombardy, Italy (75cl, 12.50%)
100% Chardonnay (6.1g RS)
Delicately refined, spiced and toasty aromatics lead into a crisp palate that is bursting with luscious fruit. A fine, slender structure, good linearity and a nicely dry finish. **$$ per bottle**

FRATELLI BERLUCCHI

GOLD

Casa delle Colonne 2009 Brut
Franciacorta DOCG, Lombardy, Italy (75cl, 13%)
80% Chardonnay, 20% Pinot Noir (6.8g RS)
Deeply evolved aromas of wax and honey with a complexing nuttiness. Full-bodied on the palate, with dried fruit emerging. Great toastiness, long and fruity. **$$$$ per bottle**

SILVER

Fratelli Berlucchi 2011 Freccianera Brut

Franciacorta DOCG, Lombardy, Italy (75cl, 12.50%)
60% Chardonnay, 30% Pinot Bianco, 10% Pinot Noir (6.1g RS)
Some bronze tints with a very mellow, toasty-oaky nose. Austere linear palate, long with a dry brut finish. **$$$ per bottle**

SILVER

Fratelli Berlucchi 2012 Freccianera Nature

Franciacorta DOCG, Lombardy, Italy (75cl, 12.50%)
85% Chardonnay, 15% Pinot Noir (1.2g RS)
Pretty damn good for a non-dosage. Youthful candle wax and floral nose, soft yet crisp and zingy fruit on the palate. **$$$ per bottle**

GOLD

Fratelli Berlucchi 2012 Freccianera Satèn

Franciacorta DOCG, Lombardy, Italy (75cl, 12.50%)
100% Chardonnay (6.3g RS)

- Best Franciacorta Future Release

Lightly toasted, yeast-complexed aromas leading to a big, creamy, oaky-toasty palate balanced by acidity and zesty fruit, ending with a lovely soft brut finish. **$$$ per bottle**

GOLD

Freccianera 2012 Rosa

Franciacorta DOCG, Lombardy, Italy (75cl, 12.50%)
40% Chardonnay, 60% Pinot Noir (6g RS)
Pale-salmon colour, attractively perfumed Pinot aromas, super-succulent, fresh and vibrant fruit make this Franciacorta very easy to drink, but it is very classy at the same time. **$$$ per bottle**

FREIXENET

SILVER

Freixenet Elyssia NV Gran Cuvée de Prestige

Cava DO, Spain (75cl, 12%)
37% Parellada, 32% Macabeo, 21% Chardonnay, 10% Pinot Noir (9g RS)
Pale-lemon colour. A beautifully smooth, sleek, modern Cava that tapers to a lovely dry finish. **$$ per bottle**

FURLEIGH ESTATE

SILVER

Furleigh Estate 2010 English Brut Rosé

Dorset, England (75cl, 12%)
60% Chardonnay, 35% Pinot Noir, 5% Meunier (12g RS)
Mid-peach colour. Crisp and spicy, with lovely succulent fruit and a fine balanced length. **$$$ per bottle**

G.H. MUMM

GOLD

Mumm 2002 R. Lalou Brut
Champagne, France (75cl, 12.50%)
53% Pinot Noir, 47% Chardonnay (6g RS)
This is an exceptional, Pinot-dominated, mature vintage, with supple and harmonious yeast-complexed aromas, a creamy mousse and a full, round and powerfully intense palate that deserves to be accompanied by food.
$$$$$ per bottle

GOLD

Mumm 2006 Brut Le Millésimé (Magnum)
Champagne, France (150cl, 12.50%)
36% Chardonnay, 64% Pinot Noir (6g RS)
Deep evolving nose with Pinot aromas dominating and complexed by notes of spice and pastry. A lovely, elegant style with delicate fruit over a firm, pin-cushion mousse and a nicely tapering finish. **$$$ per magnum**

GOLD

Mumm NV Blanc de Blancs de Cramant (Magnum)
Champagne, France (150cl, 12%)
100% Chardonnay (6g RS)
This is precision winemaking by any standards, produced from extraordinarily high quality grapes, both in terms of vintage (although this is non-vintage) and vineyard. A great quality Champagne that shows exceptional finesse, intense, linear fruit and great minerality. Such finesse! And it is only increased by the sumptuousness of its pin-cushion mousse.
$$$$ per magnum

SILVER

Mumm NV Cordon Rouge
Champagne, France (75cl, 12%)
45% Pinot Noir, 25% Meunier, 30% Chardonnay (8g RS)
Fresh, ripe yellow apple and peach aroma with light notes of yeast-aged complexity. Lovely fresh fruit on the palate, softened by a sumptuous mousse. **$$$ per bottle**

GOLD

Mumm NV Cordon Rouge (Magnum)
Champagne, France (150cl, 12%)
45% Pinot Noir, 25% Meunier, 30% Chardonnay (8g RS)
"This must be a magnum!" wrote one judge and what a difference a magnum makes. Gorgeously refined nose with sweet, super pure fruitiness and lovely lightly toasted lining. Feather-light fruit of impressive intensity. Lovely fresh, silky-softy, linear palate with succulent, lengthy, juicy, mouth-watering fruit. Lovely creamy complexity. **$$$ per magnum**

SILVER

Mumm NV Demi Sec
Champagne, France (75cl, 12%)
60% Meunier, 30% Pinot Noir, 10% Chardonnay (40g RS)
Soft, fruit-forward aromas followed by plenty of sweet, candied, grapey fruit. Definitely at the sweet end of the demi-sec spectrum. **$$$ per bottle**

GOLD

Mumm NV Grand Cru Brut Selection
Champagne, France (75cl, 12%)
60% Pinot Noir, 40% Chardonnay (6g RS)
Ethereal white-fruit aromas with a delicate toastiness. The palate is mellow yet with fresh structure and a soft, creamy texture. Light in weight but intense and fruity, with the loveliest and softest od mousses. **$$$ per bottle**

GOLD

Mumm NV Grand Cru Brut Selection (Magnum)
Champagne, France (150cl, 12%)
60% Pinot Noir, 40% Chardonnay (6g RS)
Lovely, sophisticated aromas, with the barest hint of toast, and red and white fruit in a sweet, ripe, seductive, layered style. Long, soft and lingering. Such elegance and as light as a feather! **$$$ per magnum**

SILVER

Mumm NV Rosé (Magnum)
Champagne, France (150cl, 12%)
60% Pinot Noir, 22% Chardonnay, 18% Meunier (6g RS)
Medium-salmon colour with berries on the nose and deliciously fresh fruit on the palate. Elegantly well structured. **$$$ per magnum**

SILVER

Mumm 2009 Brut Le Millésimé
Champagne, France (75cl, 12.50%)
32% Chardonnay, 68% Pinot Noir (6g RS)
Soft and creamy aroma over tropical fruit, with notes of intense yeast-aged influence. Supple yet taut palate with high expression of red-fruits that taper to a long, creamy finish. **$$$ per bottle**

GRAHAM BECK

GOLD

Graham Beck 2009 Cuvée Clive
Cap Classique, Western Cape, South Africa (75cl, 12.20%)
80% Chardonnay, 20% Pinot Noir, None (7.4g RS)

- Best South African Brut Blend
- Best South African Sparkling Wine

Gunpowder Chardonnay; fine, rich and explosive, as one judge succinctly put it! Exuberantly toasty-fruit with notes of coffee. **$$ per bottle**

SILVER

GRAHAM BECK 2010 ROSÉ

Cap Classique, Western Cape, South Africa (75cl, 12.20%)
80% Pinot Noir, 20% Chardonnay, None (6.1g RS)
Lovely, pale-salmon colour, with peach aromas and complex, softly oxidative notes of sweet marmalade. Still energetic on the palate. Has a lovely crisp fruit expression and the flavour lingers. **$$ per bottle**

GRAMONA

SILVER

ENOTECA GRAMONA 2001 FINCA DE L'ORIGEN NATURE

Cava DO, Catalunya, Spain (75cl, 12.50%)
75% Xarel-lo, 25% Macabeo (0.5g RS)
A deep, bright and resonating golden colour, this Cava has gorgeous vanilla fruit with lot's of aged depth and charred, toasty notes, followed by a tight palate that is packed with full, fleshy and succulent vanilla-laden fruit. We had to open all four bottles to find this one, the other three all being corked to one degree or another. [Not only does this Cava go through a hugely extended time on yeast, but it also does so under cork, not crown-cap.]
$$$$$ per bottle

GOLD

GRAMONA 2005 CELLER BATLLE

Cava DO, Catalunya, Spain (75cl, 12%)
75% Xarel-lo, 25% Macabeo (4g RS)
As one judge wrote "Classic Gramona style!" [The most Marmite brand of sparkling wine in the world] Mid-lemon colour, sweet vanilla-scented nose with a touch of lift and hefty woodiness coming through. **$$$$ per bottle**

GREMILLET

GOLD

BLANC DE NOIRS NV BLANC DE NOIRS

Champagne, France (75cl, 12%)
100% Pinot Noir (10g RS)

- Best Champagne Blanc de Noirs

Soft and mellow, youthfully fresh aromas, followed by plush, soft, creamy and elegant fruit on the palate, with a lovely, crisp finish. **$$$ per bottle**

GRUET WINERY

SILVER

GRUET WINERY NV BLANC DE NOIRS

New Mexico, USA (75cl, 12%)
75% Pinot Noir, 25% Chardonnay (10g RS)
Pale-peach colour. Delicately exuberant fruit aromas, with fresh, zesty fruit on palate. This is a pretty sparkling wine that showcases fine Pinot character. Delightful and easy-drinking. **$$ per bottle**

GUIDO BERLUCCHI

SILVER

BERLUCCHI '61 2009 NATURE

Franciacorta DOCG, Lombardy, Italy (75cl, 12.50%)
80% Chardonnay, 20% Pinot Noir (0g RS)
The fruit aromas are ripe and show some complexity. On the palate there is plenty of ripe fruit, with developed notes of toast and nuts. A bit big and chunky perhaps, but it has the structure to take it. **$$$ per bottle**

SILVER

BERLUCCHI '61 2009 NATURE (MAGNUM)

Franciacorta DOCG, Lombardy, Italy (150cl, 12.50%)
80% Chardonnay, 20% Pinot Noir (0g RS)
Fine toasty aroma with sumptuous fruit that is so succulent that it finishes despite being a brut nature. Lovely, fresh, long, lingering, lemony fruit. Crisp and tapering. **$$$ per magnum**

GOLD

BERLUCCHI '61 NV BRUT

Franciacorta DOCG, Lombardy, Italy (75cl, 12.50%)
90% Chardonnay, 10% Pinot Noir (7g RS)

- Best Franciacorta NV Blend

A refined, yeast-complexed aroma with the barest hint of toast emerging. Fresh, long and linear with a fine, succulent palate and a creamy, tapering finish. **$$$ per bottle**

GOLD

BERLUCCHI '61 NV BRUT (MAGNUM)

Franciacorta DOCG, Lombardy, Italy (150cl, 12.50%)
90% Chardonnay, 10% Pinot Noir (7g RS)
Lovely yeast-complexed, toast-laden aromas with notes of vanilla and ripe fruit. Light and lively in the mouth. Lovely mousse. Crisp and zingy with a very creamy, long finish. **$$$ per magnum**

SILVER

BERLUCCHI '61 NV ROSÉ

Franciacorta DOCG, Lombardy, Italy (75cl, 12.50%)
40% Chardonnay, 60% Pinot Noir (8g RS)
Pale-to-medium peach colour, with a deep, fresh, red-fruit aroma and a rich and lingering palate. Smooth textured. A good food wine. **$$$ per bottle**

GOLD

Berlucchi '61 NV Rosé (Magnum)
Franciacorta DOCG, Lombardy, Italy (150cl, 12.50%)
40% Chardonnay, 60% Pinot Noir (8g RS)

- Best Franciacorta NV Rosé
- Best Franciacorta Magnum, Best Franciacorta

Strikingly starbright pale-salmon colour, this wine exudes fine aromatics, with pastry complexity and gunpowder notes. This is a wine that is oozing fruit on the palate, but it is very fine fruit, thanks to the silky finesse of its mousse. Some aged complexity . Very long and sophisticated, with an excellent dry brut finish. Nice acid line adds freshness, vitality and purity. **$$$ per magnum**

GOLD

Berlucchi '61 NV Satèn
Franciacorta DOCG, Lombardy, Italy (75cl, 12.50%)
100% Chardonnay (8g RS)
An elegant, toast-lined aroma with cool, white fruit, peaches, yellow apple and vanilla following onto palate, which is creamy and balanced by lemon and key lime fruit. Gently caressed by a fluffy mousse, this wine has a lovely acid line and a long, tapering finish. **$$$ per bottle**

SILVER

Berlucchi '61 NV Satèn (Magnum)
Franciacorta DOCG, Lombardy, Italy (150cl, 12.50%)
100% Chardonnay (8g RS)
Absolutely gorgeous fruit sitting on a soft, fluffy, sumptuous cushiony mousse. Ripe, almost too ripe fruit. Big and plush. **$$$ per magnum**

GOLD

Guido Berlucchi NV Cuvée Imperiale Brut (Magnum)
Franciacorta DOCG, Lombardy, Italy (150cl, 12.50%)
90% Chardonnay, 10% Pinot Noir (8g RS)
Mid-lemon colour. Soft, fresh and smooth, age-mellowed aromas leading to rich, complex, creamy fruit on the palate, buttressed by a freshness of pin-cushion mousse. **$$$ per magnum**

GUSBOURNE

SILVER

Gusbourne 2013 Brut Réserve
Kent, England (75cl, 12%)
55% Pinot Noir, 27% Meunier, 18% Chardonnay (9g RS)

Soft, toast-laden aroma with gentle notes of spicy complexity. Nicely structured palate of lovely, fresh and balanced, Pinot-dominated fruit. **$$$ per bottle**

SILVER
Gusbourne 2013 Rosé
Kent, England (75cl, 12%)
100% Pinot Noir (9g RS)
Light Anjou Rosé colour, plush red berry aromas with some developed notes. Fresh, scintillating, zingy, with a smooth and silky texture. **$$$ per bottle**

HAMBLEDON VINEYARD

SILVER
Hambledon NV Classic Cuvée
Hampshire, England (75cl, 12%)
70% Chardonnay, 20% Pinot Noir, 10% Meunier (8g RS)
Soft, fruit-forward red-fruit aromas, despite the Chardonnay-dominated mix of this blend. Some complex, mature notes. A plush, fleshy palate with high acidity and rich, slowly-evolving fruit. **$$$ per bottle**

SILVER
Hambledon NV Premiere Cuvée
Hampshire, England (75cl, 12%)
58% Chardonnay, 24% Pinot Noir, 18% Meunier (8g RS)
Aromatics of some depth and maturity, with some barrel-ferment notes that follow onto the rich and complex, crisp and zingy palate. **$$$ per bottle**

HATTINGLEY VALLEY

GOLD
Hattingley Valley 2011 Blanc de Blancs
England (75cl, 12%)
100% Chardonnay (9g RS)
- Best English Future Release

A finely nuanced nose with white-fruit and notes of mild spice. Lovely mousse, gorgeous bright orchard fruits underscored by zingy acids that tapers to clean brut finish. **$$$ per bottle**

SILVER
Hattingley Valley 2013 Classic Cuvée
England (75cl, 12%)
49% Chardonnay, 33% Pinot Noir, 16% Meunier, 2% Pinot Gris (9g RS)
Big nose with a lovely palate of sappy, juicy fruit. Plush and more on the red-fruit side. Long. **$$$ per bottle**

GOLD
Hattingley Valley 2013 Classic Cuvée (Magnum)
England (150cl, 12%)
49% Chardonnay, 33% Pinot Noir, 16% Meunier, 2% Pinot Gris (9g RS)
Fresh, zippy, pineapple fruit with a crisp, sherbety finish. Well balanced with good structure and a lovely fruit intensity. **$$$$ per magnum**

GOLD

Hattingley Valley 2013 Rosé
England (75cl, 12%)
60% Pinot Noir, 36% Meunier, 4% Pinot Noir Précoce (9g RS)

- Best English Vintaged Rosé

A lovely pale-pink colour, youthful aroma followed by super-zesty fruit. So elegant, so fine. Truly delightful. **$$$ per bottle**

HENRI ABELÉ

SILVER

Henri Abelé NV Blanc de Blancs
Champagne, France (75cl, 12%)
100% Chardonnay (8g RS)
Fresh, light and easy-going, with a fragrant, soft fruit-forward aroma. A succulent and creamy palate, full of fresh, opulent fruitiness with an underlying zingy acidity that give this Champagne its quaffing character. **$$$ per bottle**

HENRIOT

SILVER

Blanc de Blancs NV Blanc de Blancs
Champagne, France (75cl, 12%)
100% Chardonnay (7g RS)
Some chalky complexity over a creamy palate with a good, fluffy mousse, this is a slightly oxidative Champagne that has enough richness, complexity and precision finish to make it a worthy Silver medal winner. **$$$ per bottle**

GOLD

Henriot 2006 Brut Millésime
Champagne, France (75cl, 12%)
50% Chardonnay, 50% Pinot Noir (7g RS)
A creamy-caramel, vanilla-laden nose, showing lots of ageing-depth, with complexing notes of honey, brioche and dried fruits. Forward and generous with more than enough freshness. Instantly impressive and ready to drink now. **$$$ per bottle**

GOLD

Henriot 2008 Rosé Millésime
Champagne, France (75cl, 12%)
45% Chardonnay, 55% Pinot Noir (8g RS)
Lovely pale peachy colour. Stylishly developed toasty aromas with lots of yeast-complexed fruity notes. Soft, fresh, delicious and sophisticated, this is a refined, crisp and linear Champagne with lovely concentration of fruit providing a lingering, polished finish. **$$$ per bottle**

SILVER

HENRIOT NV BRUT SOUVERAIN

Champagne, France (75cl, 12%)
50% Chardonnay, 45% Pinot Noir, 5% Meunier (7g RS)
Toasty aromas with complex notes of tropical fruit, marmalade and cardamom. Creamy-sweet, yeast-complexed fruit on the palate with a good brut balance and a lingering, plump finish. **$$$ per bottle**

HENRY OF PELHAM

SILVER

HENRY OF PELHAM CUVÉE CATHARINE 2011 ESTATE BLANC DE BLANC CARTE BLANCH

Short Hills Bench, Niagara Peninsula, Canada (75cl, 12.50%)
100% Chardonnay (8.3g RS)
Mid-lemon colour. Creamy-caramel, butterscotch aroma, with notes of peach and honey. Fresh, zesty and vibrant with a long, succulent, brut finish. **$$$ per bottle**

HERMANN VINHOS E VINHAS

SILVER

LÍRICA NV BRUT MÉTODO CLÁSSICO

Rio Grande Do Sul, Pinheiro Machado, Brazil (75cl, 11.80%)
75% Chardonnay, 15% Gouveio, 10% Pinot Noir (8.5g RS)
Deep lemon-gold colour. Nicely restrained, soft, mellow, ripe-fruit aromas with light-toasty notes, giving way to a round, fleshy palate. Concentrated but not heavy, with a creamy, seductive finish. **$ per bottle**

HINDLEAP

SILVER

BLUEBELL VINEYARD ESTATES 2010 HINDLEAP BLANC DE BLANCS

England (75cl, 11.50%)
100% Chardonnay (11.2g RS)
Youthful pure nose. Lovely fruit mid-palate and finish. Crisp, lemony, lean and long. **$$$ per bottle**

HOUSE OF ARRAS

SILVER

HOUSE OF ARRAS 2003 EJ CARR LATE DISGORGED

Tasmania, Australia (75cl, 12.50%)
61% Chardonnay, 39% Pinot Noir (6.5g RS)
Mid-lemon colour. Honeyed, aged dried-fruit, yeast-complexed aroma follows through onto a long and succulent palate. Feels more like a wine than fizz and would have benefitted from an extra gram of dosage, but just too damn good not to get a Silver medal. **$$$$ per bottle**

GOLD

House Of Arras 2006 Blanc de Blancs

Tasmania, Australia (75cl, 12.50%)
94% Chardonnay, 5% Pinot Noir, 1% Meunier (5.8g RS)

- Best Australian Blanc de Blancs

Rich, super-toasty aromas with coffee, vanilla and dried-fruit complexity. So fine-tuned and polished, with such classic complexity and refreshing vibrancy, this is self-evidently the work of a master of his craft [sorry Ed, you cannot hide when you make wines like this!]. **$$$ per bottle**

GOLD

House Of Arras 2006 Rosé

Tasmania, Australia (75cl, 12.50%)
65% Pinot Noir, 33% Chardonnay, 2% Meunier (6.5g RS)

- Best Australian Vintaged Rosé

Very pale copper-hued colour with delicate peach aroma and super-smooth toasty notes. Although not big fans of noticeable oak in sparkling wines, we all admired the lovely oak impact here. **$$$ per bottle**

GOLD

House Of Arras 2007 Grand Vintage

Tasmania, Australia (75cl, 12.50%)
78% Chardonnay, 22% Pinot Noir (6.7g RS)
Mid-lemon colour, with deep, expressive charred notes pervading the very fruity aromatics, and a fine, fresh palate of zingy, concentrated fruit , with a long, tight, brut finish. **$$$ per bottle**

GOLD

House Of Arras NV A by Arras

Tasmania, Australia (75cl, 12.50%)
59% Pinot Noir, 33% Chardonnay, 8% Meunier (11g RS)

- Best Australian NV Blend
- Best Value Australian Sparkling Wine

Pale-lemon in colour with slowly evolving white-fruit aromas that are only just starting to build complexity. A creamy palate that is both crisp and smooth, with a lovely long and soft, brut-driven finish. **$$ per bottle**

SILVER

House Of Arras NV Brut Elite C801

Tasmania, Australia (75cl, 12.50%)
55% Pinot Noir, 43% Chardonnay, 2% Meunier (9.2g RS)
Pale-lemon colour. Restrained, fresh, young and ripe white-fruit aroma with complexing notes of floral-toast and baking spices. Brilliant freshness and overflowing with soft, ripe, sun-kissed fruit that carries to a fresh brut finish. Very clever use of barrel-ferment, reserve wines and dosage to produce a youthfully complex sparkling wine. **$$ per bottle**

HOWARD PARK WINES

SILVER

HOWARD PARK JETÉ NV BRUT
Western Australia, Australia (75cl, 12%)
84% Chardonnay, 16% Pinot Noir (6g RS)
Mid-lemon colour. Toasty-gunpowder aroma, with rich, ripe and tasty fruit on a slender structure, with super acidity at the finish. **$$$ per bottle**

HUNTER'S

GOLD

HUNTER'S MIRUMIRU™ 2011 RESERVE
Marlborough, New Zealand (75cl, 12.50%)
55% Pinot Noir, 42% Chardonnay, 3% Meunier (6.7g RS)

- Best New Zealand Vintaged Brut Blend

Intense lemon colour, full of rich, complex, yeasty-toasty aromas followed by lovely fruit on the palate, with a soft creaminess on aftertaste. Intelligent blending and use of malolactic. Nice leesy and autolytic undertone. Crisp and classy palate, with a lovely firm and fruity brut finish. **$$$ per bottle**

GOLD

HUNTER'S MIRUMIRU™ NV ROSÉ
Marlborough, New Zealand (75cl, 12.50%)
55% Pinot Noir, 41% Chardonnay, 4% Meunier (7.5g RS)

- Best New Zealand Rosé
- Best New Zealand Sparkling Wine

The prettiest, clearest, pale pink-pink rosé colour. Lightly complexed red-fruit aroma. Gorgeous, polished, wild strawberry fruit on palate. Mouth-watering and squeaky-clean. Gold medal by any standard. **$$ per bottle**

HUSH HEATH ESTATE

SILVER

BALFOUR LESLIE'S RESERVE NV EXTRA DRY
Kent, England (75cl, 12%)
55% Pinot Noir, 40% Chardonnay, 5% Meunier, None (17g RS)
Soft, peachy fruit aroma with a hint of peardrops, a classy, round palate and a soft mousse. **$$$ per bottle**

JACQUART

SILVER

JACQUART 2008 VINTAGE
Champagne, France (75cl, 12.50%)
50% Chardonnay, 50% Pinot Noir (8g RS)
This Champagne might lack the wow-factor, but it has everything required for a top Silver, from its super-ripe aroma of dried fruits, apricots and nuts to is creamy palate. **$$$ per bottle**

SILVER

Jacquart NV Brut Mosaïque (Magnum)
Champagne, France (150cl, 12.50%)
40% Chardonnay, 35% Pinot Noir, 25% Meunier (9g RS)
Fresh orchard aromas and flavours polished by what feels like lovely magnum finesse. Classy and classic, extremely elegant, fresh, yeast-complexed fruit on palate. **$$$ per magnum**

GOLD

Jacquart NV Brut Mosaïque Rosé
Champagne, France (75cl, 12.50%)
45% Pinot Noir, 34% Chardonnay, 21% Meunier (8.5g RS)
Fine pink-bronze colour leading to a gorgeous fruit aroma, deliciously yeast-complexed fruit on the palate and a sumptuous, fluffy mousse. Long and easy drinking. **$$$ per bottle**

JANSZ TASMANIA

GOLD

Jansz Tasmania 2010 Vintage Cuvée
Tasmania, Australia (75cl, 12.50%)
51% Pinot Noir, 49% Chardonnay (6.5g RS)
Pale-lemon colour, with a complex, stylishly evolved toasty aroma leading to classic gunpowder fruit and lean structure. Powerful, persistent and really quite macho. **$$$ per bottle**

GOLD

Jansz Tasmania NV Premium Rosé
Tasmania, Australia (75cl, 12%)
84% Pinot Noir, 15% Chardonnay, 1% Meunier (8.7g RS)

- Best Australian NV Rosé

Fabulously pale pink-pink colour, with refined, delicate red-fruit aromatics, and a fresh, creamy palate of soft, youthful fruit that carries to a soft brut finish with a pithy aftertaste. **$$ per bottle**

JENKYN PLACE

SILVER

Jenkyn Place 2010 Blanc de Noir
Hampshire, England (75cl, 11.40%)
50% Pinot Noir, 50% Meunier (9g RS)
This style is rarely produced in England. It is pale in colour with a light, refined and youthful nose, followed by crisp, balanced, nicely expressive Pinot fruity. **$$$ per bottle**

SILVER

Jenkyn Place 2010 Brut

Hampshire, England (75cl, 11.80%)

60% Chardonnay, 32% Pinot Noir, 8% Meunier (8g RS)

Classy restrained nose. Lovely, fresh, vibrant and zippy. Long with tight acid drive. **$$$ per bottle**

JOSEPH PERRIER

SILVER

Joseph Perrier 2008 Cuvée Royale Blanc de Noirs Vintage

Champagne, France (75cl, 12%)

100% Pinot Noir (3g RS)

Plush, spiced, red-fruit aroma and smooth, velvety palate of rich, powerful, round and fleshy Pinot flavour. Needs to be cellared for another two years at least. **$$$ per bottle**

JUVÉ Y CAMPS

SILVER

Juvé y Camps 2006 La Capella

Cava DO, Penedès, Spain (75cl, 12%)

100% Xarel-lo (2.7g RS)

A 10 year old top quality traditional Xarel-lo in this preserved condition is hard to find. Mid-lemon in colour with an age-complexed, spicy aroma that carries through to the palate, which is lifted by a silky mousse for additional finesse. **$$$$ per bottle**

SILVER

Juvé y Camps 2010 Gran Reserva

Cava DO, Penedès, Spain (75cl, 12%)

40% Xarel-lo, 25% Macabeo, 25% Chardonnay, 10% Parellada (7.8g RS)

Mid-lemon in colour with an oxidative aroma, but more restrained and voluminous on palate, which is creamy and has lovely, fresh fruit, a sumptuous mousse and a soft finish. **$$$ per bottle**

SILVER

Juvé y Camps 2013 Selección Reserva

Cava DO, Penedès, Spain (75cl, 12%)

34% Xarel-lo, 33% Macabeo, 33% Parellada (8.6g RS)

Pale-lemon in colour, with an attractive, harmonious, stylishly spicy aroma followed by an intense palate, which is clean, crisp with a soft and elegant finish. **$$ per bottle**

GOLD

JUVÉ Y CAMPS CINTA PÚRPURA 2012 BRUT RESERVA
Cava DO, Penedès, Spain (75cl, 12%)
34% Xarel-lo, 33% Macabeo, 33% Parellada (7.8g RS)

- Best Cava Future Release

Mid-lemon colour. Mild, soft and creamy white-fruit aroma with gentle spicy notes. Attractively soft and vibrant fruit on the palate, which is beautifully structured with lovely acidity providing a crisp and long finish.
$$ per bottle

SILVER

JUVÉ Y CAMPS NV SWEET RESERVA
Cava DO, Penedès, Spain (75cl, 12%)
34% Xarel-lo, 33% Macabeo, 33% Parellada (52g RS)
Pale-lemon colour with a fine and delicately sweet grapiness on the nose. The palate is very soft with a lovely sweetness and excellent sugar balance, but it needs to be cellared for 12-18 months to come together. **$$ per bottle**

KREINBACHER

GOLD

KREINBACHER 2011 BRUT CLASSIC (MAGNUM)
Somló, Somló-Hegy, Hungary (150cl, 12%)
100% Furmint (11.1g RS)

- Best Hungarian Blanc de Blancs
- Best Hungarian Magnum
- Best Hungarian Sparkling Wine

This wine has a bright, lemon-gold colour, a nicely autolytic nose with pastry and toasty richness over opulent fruit of absolutely glacial evolution, and a gorgeous vanilla flick of potential complexity on the finish. Would love to age this anther 3-5 years! **$$$ per magnum**

GOLD

KREINBACHER NV PRESTIGE BRUT
Somló, Somló-Hegy, Hungary (75cl, 12.50%)
100% Furmint (8.6g RS)
Mid-lemon colour. Very young, yet has emerging complex toasty aromas. Really quite nice now with a lovely mousse that is so soft and creamy, but has acidity and structure to age well. **$$ per bottle**

LA MONTINA

SILVER

LA MONTINA 2009 MILLESIMATO BRUT
Franciacorta DOCG, Lombardy, Italy (75cl, 12%)
60% Chardonnay, 40% Pinot Noir (8g RS)
Ripe, mature, fruity aromas and a creamy palate with lovely spicy-citrus fruit complexity that carries to a long, firm brut finish. **$$$ per bottle**

SILVER

La Montina NV Satèn Brut
Franciacorta DOCG, Lombardy, Italy (75cl, 12%)
100% Chardonnay (7g RS)
A pronounced, evolving aroma of ripe fruit with a light, toasty complexity. Round and plush on the palate, which has nicely piquant fruit and tapers to a gentle lift on the finish. **$$$ per bottle**

LANSON

GOLD

Lanson 2004 Gold Label 2004 (Magnum)
Champagne, France (150cl, 12.50%)
52% Pinot Noir, 48% Chardonnay (8g RS)
Classic high-acid style that has remained extremely youthful. Fresh and zesty, yet round and rich with succulent, honey-laden fruit that is very slowly building up complexity and ideal for cellaring. **$$$ per magnum**

GOLD

Lanson 2008 Gold Label Brut
Champagne, France (75cl, 12.50%)
53% Pinot Noir, 47% Chardonnay (7g RS)
Exceptionally stylish, spice-laden and intensely fruity aromas that are evolving so glacially that it will take eons to achieve its true potential complexity. Although this is a big wine in every sense, it is also impressively linear-driven with a palate that is brimming with truly sumptuous fruit and such an extraordinary acid-line, even for a 2008, that it seemingly tapers into infinity. Such great potential here that I would have no hesitation laying it down for a decade. **$$$ per bottle**

GOLD

Lanson Cuvée Père et Fils NV Brut
Champagne, France (75cl, 12.50%)
45% Pinot Noir, 35% Chardonnay, 20% Meunier (6g RS)
Soft, overt, spiced-apple and maturing Pinot aromatics. A creamy palate of lovely, fresh and fleshy, yeast-complexed fruit. Good intensity and a lingering flavour. **$$$ per bottle**

GOLD

Lanson NV Black Label Brut (Magnum)
Champagne, France (150cl, 12.50%)
50% Pinot Noir, 35% Chardonnay, 15% Meunier (8g RS)
Lightly yeast-complexed aromas with lovely overlaying toasty notes Gorgeous fruit with fleshy structure and a lovely acid attack on the finish. Juicy and succulent. **$$$$ per magnum**

SILVER

LANSON NV ROSE LABEL BRUT ROSÉ (MAGNUM)
Champagne, France (150cl, 12.50%)
53% Pinot Noir, 32% Chardonnay, 15% Meunier (8g RS)
This has class! Not just fruit, but exquisite creamy-yeast-complexed fruit, with a sublime mousse. Really top Silver quality. **$$$$ per magnum**

SILVER

LANSON NV WHITE LABEL (MAGNUM)
Champagne, France (150cl, 12.50%)
50% Pinot Noir, 35% Chardonnay, 15% Meunier (28g RS)
Fresh, crisp and classy, with succulent marmalade fruit and not too sweet thanks to its fabulous acidity. **$$$$ per magnum**

LANTIERI

GOLD

LANTIERI 2011 ARCADIA MILLESIMATO BRUT
Franciacorta DOCG, Lombardy, Italy (75cl, 12.50%)
70% Chardonnay, 30% Pinot Noir, None (8g RS)
- Best Franciacorta Vintaged Brut Blend

Super-stylish toasty nose with gunpowdery note, succulent, fruity palate, fine linearity and long, with a very good soft brut balance. **$$$ per bottle**

SILVER

LANTIERI NV EXTRA BRUT
Franciacorta DOCG, Lombardy, Italy (75cl, 12.50%)
90% Chardonnay, 10% Pinot Noir (3g RS)
Fresh, fine and refined aromas with fresh, zingy and elegantly-rich fruit on a very creamy palate. Long and linear. Soft brut finish. **$$ per bottle**

LAURENT-PERRIER

GOLD

LAURENT-PERRIER 2004 ALEXANDRA ROSÉ
Champagne, France (75cl, 12%)
80% Pinot Noir, 20% Chardonnay (10.6g RS)
Copper-bronze colour. Extremely fine, with a powerful Pinot aroma teeming with red fruits fruit and gently nuanced toasty notes. A lively palate. Fresh and dancing on the palate. Long and juicy finish. **$$$$$ per bottle**

GOLD

LAURENT-PERRIER NV CUVÉE ROSÉ
Champagne, France (75cl, 12%)
100% Pinot Noir (12g RS)
Deepish bronze-pink colour. Restrained Pinot aroma with spiced-cherry notes. Rich on the palate and long in length, with an attractive phenolic twist at the finish. **$$$$ per bottle**

LE COLTURE

SILVER

Le Colture NV Fagher Brut

Valdobbiadene Prosecco Superiore DOCG, Veneto, Italy (75cl, 11.50%)
90% Glera, 10% Chardonnay (9g RS)
Attractive peardrop amylic aromas, with excellent mousse retention immediately visible on the surface of the wine. Soft pear, grass and peach. fruit on palate Mellow and creamy. Crisp finish. **$$ per bottle**

SILVER

Le Colture NV Pianer Extra

Valdobbiadene Prosecco Superiore DOCG, Veneto, Italy (75cl, 11%)
100% Glera (14g RS)
Very fresh, characterful nose, with deliciously soft, creamy-peachy fruit on the palate and a good dry finish. **$$ per bottle**

LE LUDE

SILVER

Le Lude NV Brut

Cap Classique, Franschhoek, Western Cape, South Africa (75cl, 8.20%)
66% Chardonnay, 34% Pinot Noir (6.5g RS)
Pale-lemon colour. Intense, yeast-complexed, yellow-fruit aromas with a full and round, soft-textured palate. Rich fruit, with lovely acids giving a line to the creamy texture, which carries to a fine brut finish. **$ per bottle**

SILVER

Le Lude NV Rosé

Cap Classique, Franschhoek, Western Cape, South Africa (75cl, 7.70%)
55% Pinot Noir, 40% Chardonnay, 5% Meunier (5.5g RS)
Lovely pale-peach colour, with spice-complexed aromas and fresh, strawberry, cherry and bitter cherry fruit on a crisp and lively palate. Well balanced. **$ per bottle**

LEGRAS & HAAS

SILVER

Legras & Haas 2012 Les Sillons Blanc de Blancs Chouilly Grand Cru

Champagne, France (75cl, 12.50%), 100% Chardonnay (6.5g RS)
Oak-dominated, ripe fruit aromas with lovely, delicate Chardonnay fruit on a full-bodied, broad palate with lovely acid line that caries to an even more delicate, very long finish. **$$$$ per bottle**

SILVER

Legras & Haas NV Chouilly Grand Cru Blanc de Blancs Brut

Champagne, France (75cl, 12.50%), 100% Chardonnay (8g RS)
Soft, fresh, white-fruit aromas. Very youthful. Nicely weighted, yet fine and delicate. This Champagne shows true elegance. **$$$ per bottle**

LOUIS ROEDERER

GOLD

Louis Roederer 2002 Cristal Brut Millésime (Magnum)
Champagne, France (150cl, 12.50%)
55% Pinot Noir, 45% Chardonnay (10g RS)

- Best Deluxe Champagne Blend
- Best Deluxe Champagne Magnum
- Best Deluxe Champagne
- Best Champagne
- Best French Sparkling Wine
- Supreme World Champion

Absolute class, so fine and refined with an endless, creamy, tapering finish. The fruit is plush, succulent and juicy, yet its perfect balance and long, linear line provides such finesse. The fruit is so vital and seductive, supported by a mousse creams and puns in the mouth. There is a sense of grace and stature to this Champagne, and a sense of glacial evolution that knocks years off of its chronological age, this surely must be made from the finest raw materials under the guiding influence of one of today's most gifted winemakers. **$$$$$ per magnum**

GOLD

Louis Roederer 2002 Cristal Brut Rosé Millésime (Magnum)
Champagne, France (150cl, 12.50%)
60% Pinot Noir, 40% Chardonnay (9g RS)

- Best Deluxe Champagne Rosé

Very pale-peach colour. Super-subtle creamy-perfumed, toasty aromas. Such complexity and harmony. Lovely velvety mousse. Super length. Feather-light yet intense, bright and so very, very long. **$$$$$ per magnum**

GOLD

Louis Roederer 2006 Cristal Brut Millésime
Champagne, France (75cl, 12.50%)
60% Pinot Noir, Chardonnay, 40% Chardonnay (9g RS)
A lovely classy toastiness overlaying opulent, bright fruit brings a lovely fragrant quality to this Champagne. It is well-built, creamy and energetic with a mellow mousse. This is a classic example of great length without significant weight. Super-smart winemaking! **$$$$$ per bottle**

GOLD

Louis Roederer 2006 Cristal Brut Rosé Millésime
Champagne, France (75cl, 12.50%)
60% Pinot Noir, 40% Chardonnay (9g RS)
Lovely perfumed-fruit aromas with the subtlest of toasty notes. A crisp Champagne that feels round in the mouth thanks to its gentle, fluffy mousse. Spicy and juicy red-fruits. Very elegant. Precision winemaking! **$$$$$ per bottle**

GOLD

LOUIS ROEDERER 2008 BRUT VINTAGE (MAGNUM)
Champagne, France (150cl, 12.50%)
70% Pinot Noir, 30% Chardonnay (9g RS)
Wow, absolutely perfect! How can such utterly delicious fruit be so complex and compelling? Classic 2008! Great, slow-evolving complexity. Must be a magnum (it was...). **$$$$$ per magnum**

GOLD

LOUIS ROEDERER 2009 BRUT ROSÉ MILLÉSIME (MAGNUM)
Champagne, France (150cl, 12.50%)
62% Pinot Noir, 38% Chardonnay (9g RS)
Elegance, finesse, freshness and beauty! A mesmerising blend of intensely mineral Pinot fruit balanced by the delicacy, freshness and tapering exquisiteness of Chardonnay. A perfect balance. **$$$$ per magnum**

GOLD

LOUIS ROEDERER 2009 BRUT VINTAGE
Champagne, France (75cl, 12.50%)
70% Pinot Noir, 30% Chardonnay (9g RS)
Discreetly fruity aroma with red-fruit dominance and soft, fruit-driven palate, nicely rounded with spiced-honey notes. **$$$$ per bottle**

GOLD

LOUIS ROEDERER 2010 BLANC DE BLANCS BRUT MILLÉSIME
Champagne, France (75cl, 12.50%)
100% Chardonnay (9g RS)

- Best Champagne Vintaged Blanc de Blancs

Fragrant, bright, white-fruit aromas with delicately toasted notes. Lovely rounded, creamy palate with ample, ripe and delicious fruit that retains its vivacity thanks to refreshing acidity. **$$$$ per bottle**

GOLD

LOUIS ROEDERER 2010 BRUT ROSÉ MILLÉSIME
Champagne, France (75cl, 12.50%)
62% Pinot Noir, 38% Chardonnay (9g RS)

- Best Champagne Vintaged Rosé
- World Champion Classic Brut Rosé

Pale-peach colour with fragrant aroma and subtle, vanilla-toastiness just beginning to emerge, followed by a superb palate of succulent, juicy Pinot-dominated fruit that is rich yet tight, long and lingering. **$$$$ per bottle**

GOLD

LOUIS ROEDERER NV BRUT PREMIER (MAGNUM)
Champagne, France (150cl, 12.50%)
40% Pinot Noir, 40% Chardonnay, 20% Meunier (10g RS)
Classic yeast-complexed aroma and text-book lean structure with crisp, long and zingy fruit on a well-cushioned mouse. Classy! **$$$ per magnum**

MADFISH WINES

SILVER

VERA'S CUVÉE NV MADFISH SPARKLING WHITE
Western Australia, Australia (75cl, 12%)
77% Chardonnay, 23% Pinot Noir, 0% (7.5g RS)
Light but lovely toasty notes over exuberant fruit aroma, followed by a plush, round, succulently fruity palate with vibrant acidity providing a juicy succulence to the fruit, which caries tightly to a long, crisp finish. **$$ per bottle**

MAELI

SILVER

MAELI 2014 SPUMANTE DOLCE
Colli Euganei Fior d'Arancio DOCG, Veneto, Italy (75cl, 6%)
100% Moscato (100g RS)
A beautifully fresh, lusciously soft and cushiony texture with lovely, grapy Moscato fruitiness and a creamy mousse. Very sweet, but well balanced. **$$ per bottle**

MAILLY GRAND CRU

SILVER

MAILLY GRAND CRU L'INTEMPORELLE 2009 ROSÉ
Champagne, France (75cl, 12%)
60% Pinot Noir, 40% Chardonnay (7.9g RS)
Pale-peach colour with bronze hues, delicate peach aroma and nicely evolved, crisp, candied fruit on the palate, tapering to a good brut finish. **$$$$ per bottle**

MAS CODINA

GOLD

MAS CODINA 2013 BRUT RESERVA
Cava DO, Penedès, Spain (75cl, 12%)
45% Xarel-lo, 30% Macabeo, 15% Chardonnay, 10% Pinot Noir (10g RS)
- Best Cava Vintaged Blend

A hugely enjoyable, atypically fruity Cava for Xarel-lo as the primary variety. Mid-lemon colour, with soft, mellow white-fruit and vanilla aromatics, and a crisp palate full of bright fruit, leading to a lovely soft finish. **$ per bottle**

MASO MARTIS

GOLD

MADAME MARTIS 2006 RARE VINTAGE
Trentodoc, Trentino Alto Adige, Italy (75cl, 12.80%)
70% Pinot Noir, 25% Chardonnay, 5% Meunier (5g RS)

- Best Trentodoc Blend

This sparkling wine has big, robust and expressive aromas of vanilla and toast of some depth and quite complex, with charred notes and heaps of plush, ripe, toasty-vanilla fruit on a lovely palate, which is contrastingly slender in structure and long, tight and linear to finish. Intriguing to say the least! **$$$ per bottle**

MASOTTINA

SILVER

CONTRADA GRANDA 2015 MILLESIMATO BRUT
Conegliano-Valdobbiadene Prosecco Superiore DOCG, Veneto, Italy (75cl, 11.50%), 100% Glera (6.2g RS)
Fresh, mellow and grassy-floral aromas becoming more succulent on the palate. Long, intense and serious, finishing quite dry. **$$$ per bottle**

SILVER

MASOTTINA NV EXTRA DRY
Conegliano-Valdobbiadene Prosecco Superiore DOCG, Veneto, Italy (75cl, 11.50%), 100% Glera (14g RS)
Lovely fresh peardrop fruit aromas and super-fresh, succulent fruit on the palate. A lovely, smooth. Fresh and squeaky clean. **$$ per bottle**

MIGUEL TORRES CHILE

SILVER

CORDILLERA NV BRUT BLANC DE NOIR
Valle de Curicó, Central Valley, Chile (75cl, 12%)
100% Pinot Noir (6g RS)
Pale-lemon colour. Clean, fresh, restrained aroma following onto the palate, which is full of energy. Neatly made, fruit-forward and easy-going with impressive Pinot character that carries to soft brut finish. **$$ per bottle**

GOLD

SANTA DIGNA ESTELADO ROSÉ NV UVA PAÏS
Secano Interior, Central Valley, Chile (75cl, 12%), 100% Païs (8g RS)

- Best Chilean Rosé
- Best Chilean Organic
- Best Chilean Sparkling Wine
- World Champion Brut from a non-classic grape

Exquisitely pale peach colour, elegantly restrained nose, with cool, linear strawberry fruit, finishing with an attractive lemony bite. **$ per bottle**

MOËT & CHANDON

GOLD

MCIII NV Moët & Chandon 001.14
Champagne, France (75cl, 12.50%)
45% Pinot Noir, 45% Chardonnay, 10% Meunier (5g RS)
Chairman's Trophy
An absolutely spellbinding blend of great reserve wines. Immaculate. Full-on soft, spicy, complex aromas of apricot, meadow flowers and honey with evolved pastry notes. Lovely spiciness, very complex, overflowing with reserve wine mellowness and richness, caressed by the beautiful, velvety sweetness of mature wine. **$$$$$ per bottle**

GOLD

Moët & Chandon 1998 Grand Vintage Collection
Champagne, France (75cl, 12.50%)
35% Pinot Noir, 25% Meunier, 40% Chardonnay (5g RS)

- Best Champagne Future Release (re-release)

Lovely, bright, toast-laden aroma with notes of gunpowdery complexity following through onto the palate, which is brisk and creamy, long and linear. **$$$$ per bottle**

GOLD

Moët & Chandon 2006 Grand Vintage (Magnum)
Champagne, France (150cl, 12.50%)
42% Chardonnay, 39% Pinot Noir, 19% Meunier (5g RS)

- Best Champagne Vintaged Blend
- Best Champagne Vintaged Magnum
- World Champion Classic Vintaged Brut Blend

Judging is not about guessing. In fact, guessing can play havoc with the supposedly objective task of quality assessment under blind conditions, as it introduces an element of subjective bias. However, the Moët gunpowder style is so alive in this wine that it stood out like firework night for everyone. The aromas are very youthful, despite the gunpowdery sulphidic complexity, and this youthfulness is followed on the palate, which is brimming with lovely, sweet, pure fruitiness that is creamy and caressing, lingering in the gentlest manner. While 2006 might not be a truly great vintage, this magnum of 2006 is without doubt a truly great Champagne. **$$$$$ per magnum**

SILVER

Moët & Chandon 2008 Grand Vintage Rosé
Champagne, France (75cl, 12.50%)
46% Pinot Noir, 32% Chardonnay, 22% Meunier (5g RS)
A Tavel Rosé colour, but fresh and lovely aroma of soft red-fruit, particularly strawberry. Luscious strawberry. Almost burgundian. **$$$$ per bottle**

MONT MARÇAL

GOLD

EXTREMARIUM DE MONT MARÇAL NV BRUT RESERVA
Cava DO, Spain (75cl, 12%)
35% Xarel-lo, 25% Macabeo, 20% Parellada, 20% Chardonnay (8g RS)
Pale-lemon colour. Lovely traditional cava style, much smoother, richer than most. Absolutely fresh and clean. Fresh, vibrant with green fruit. Lovely succulent palate. **$$ per bottle**

MONTAUDON

SILVER

MONTAUDON NV BLANC DE NOIRS
Champagne, France (75cl, 12.50%)
100% Pinot Noir (10g RS)
Open red-fruit aroma. Fresh, elegant, long sweet, chewy fruit on a taut palate. Long structure with a nice, dry'ish finish. **$$$ per bottle**

SILVER

MONTAUDON NV RÉSERVE PREMIÈRE BRUT
Champagne, France (75cl, 12.50%)
50% Pinot Noir, 30% Chardonnay, 20% Meunier (11g RS)
Soft, vanilla-dusted, sweet fruit aroma, followed by ample, fruit-forward palate, full in body and with muscle. Big, bold and long.. **$$$ per bottle**

MUSCÀNDIA

GOLD

MUSCÀNDIA 2010 GRAN RESERVA NATURE
Cava DO, Catalunya, Spain (75cl, 11.50%)
80% Xarel-lo, 10% Macabeo, 10% Parellada (2g RS)
Modern style Xarel-lo. Mid-lemon colour with a youthful, fruit-forward fruit profile, just beginning to pick up yeast-complexing character. Crisp and fresh. Lovely spiciness and not as phenolic as the more traditional Xarel-lo wines. **$$ per bottle**

NICOLAS FEUILLATTE

SILVER

MILLÉSIME 2008 BRUT MILLÉSIME
Champagne, France (75cl, 12%)
20% Chardonnay, 40% Pinot Noir, 40% Meunier (8g RS)
Cool fruity aroma with delicate floral, white-fruit notes. Extremely crisp, vibrant palate with long citric acid-line providing a lovely pure fruitiness with energising tension. **$$$ per bottle**

NINO FRANCO

GOLD

Nino Franco 2015 Primo Franco

Valdobbiadene Prosecco Superiore DOCG, Veneto, Italy (75cl, 10.50%)
100% Glera (28g RS)

- Best Prosecco Dry

Floral-spice aromatics, with notes of spice that come singing through on the (not too sweet) sweetness of the palate, which is gently buttressed by a light, fluffy and voluminous mousse. For Prosecco, this is the complete package. **$$$ per bottle**

GOLD

Nino Franco 2015 Vigneto della Riva di San Floriano

Valdobbiadene Prosecco Superiore DOCG (Rive), Veneto, Italy (75cl, 12%)
100% Glera (10g RS)

- Best Prosecco Vintaged Brut

Spicy-peppery fruit, beautifully balanced, lovely depth and carry through. Long, crisp and energetic. Long on flavour. **$$ per bottle**

SILVER

Nino Franco NV Brut

Valdobbiadene Prosecco Superiore DOCG, Veneto, Italy (75cl, 11%)
100% Glera (10g RS)

Spice-laden aromas follow onto the palate, where they are magnified into a strong, white-pepperiness the pervades the fruit. Lovely soft mousse, nice fresh acidity and an authentically dry brut finish. **$$ per bottle**

GOLD

Nino Franco NV Rustico

Valdobbiadene Prosecco Superiore DOCG, Veneto, Italy (75cl, 11%)
100% Glera (11g RS)

- Best Prosecco NV Brut
- Best Prosecco

Light spicy aromatics, with peppery-spicy white fruits on the palate. Soft and gentle flavours that carry well to a crisp dry finish. **$ per bottle**

NO 1 FAMILY ESTATE

GOLD

No 1 Assemblé NV Brut

Marlborough, New Zealand (75cl, 12.50%)
60% Pinot Noir, 40% Chardonnay (10g RS)

- Best New Zealand NV Brut Blend

Pale-lemon in colour, with fresh, vibrant, ripe orchard fruit aromas. This is a lovely Pinot-dominated blend that shows more pure Pinot fruit than some pure varietal Pinot wines and such glossy, bright fruit too. Finesse and class!
$$$ per bottle

NYETIMBER

GOLD

NYETIMBER 2009 CLASSIC CUVÉE (MAGNUM)
West Sussex, England (150cl, 12%)
55% Chardonnay, 26% Pinot Noir, 19% Meunier, 0% (9g RS)
Absolutely gorgeous! The magnum effect is evident on the nose, thanks to its slowly evolving toasty aromas. Crisp fruit with notes of toast and brioche gently supported by a lovely, ultra-soft, magnum mousse. **$$$$ per magnum**

GOLD

NYETIMBER 2010 TILLINGTON SINGLE VINEYARD
West Sussex, England (75cl, 12%)
78% Pinot Noir, 22% Chardonnay, 0% 0% (9.5g RS)
Classic, complex, yeast-aged, Pinot-dominated sparkling wine of the highest order. Long, complete and stylish. Drink now or keep perfectly cellared for 10 years. **$$$$ per bottle**

ORIOL ROSSELL

SILVER

ORIOL ROSSELL CUVÉE ESPECIAL 2014 BRUT
Cava DO, Spain (75cl, 11.50%)
70% Xarel-lo, 20% Macabeo, 10% Parellada (0.5g RS)
Pale-lemon colour. Soft, fruity aroma with tropical notes, with fresh, totally pristine, peach fruit and undertones of yellow plum on the palate. Crisp and zesty, with lovely acidity and a nice phenolic flick on the finish. Carries evenly to a fresh, nicely dry finish. **$$$ per bottle**

SILVER

ORIOL ROSSELL RESERVA DE LA PROPIETAT 2010 BRUT NATURE
Cava DO, Spain (75cl, 12%)
70% Xarel-lo, 20% Macabeo, 10% Parellada (0.2g RS)
Deep lemon-gold colour, with full, round, aged and toasty aromas. Plush, soft and mouthfilling palate, which boasts a lovely mellowed evolution. Stylish. **$$$ per bottle**

PALMER & CO

GOLD

PALMER & CO 2008 VINTAGE
Champagne, France (75cl, 12%)
50% Chardonnay, 45% Pinot Noir, 5% Meunier (8g RS)
Definitely a "wow" wine! A lovely, complex, serious vintage Champagne that makes a statement. Classic lean structure, classy yeast-complexed fruit and a fine, lace-lined mousse. Super-stylish and discreetly expressive. **$$$ per bottle**

SILVER

Palmer & Co NV Blanc de Blancs Brut
Champagne, France (75cl, 12%)
100% Chardonnay (7g RS)
Overt, spiced-appley aroma over fine, precise and focused fruit on a rounded palate with a classic, creamy mousse. **$$$ per bottle**

GOLD

Palmer & Co NV Brut Réserve
Champagne, France (75cl, 12%)
50% Chardonnay, 40% Pinot Noir, 10% Meunier (8g RS)
Soft, age-complexed aroma with toasty notes. Rich, wide, fleshy palate. Fine fruit intensity and sweet, lingering length. Lovely, fresh, classy and classic. **$$$ per bottle**

PERRIER-JOUËT

GOLD

Perrier-Jouët Belle Epoque 2004 Blanc de Blancs 2004 (Magnum)
Champagne, France (150cl, 12.50%)
100% Chardonnay (8g RS)
Gunpowder aromas with ripe white fruits, and notes of spice and flowers. Big, overtly fruity, toasty-rich with mellow acidity. Surprisingly fat for a classically lean vintage like 2004. **$$$$$ per magnum**

GOLD

Perrier-Jouët Belle Epoque 2006 Rosé (Magnum)
Champagne, France (150cl, 12.50%)
45% Chardonnay, 5% Meunier, 50% Pinot Noir (8g RS)
Beautiful bronze-gold colour, with deep, toasty-peach fruit aromas and deliciously fresh and fragrant fruit on the palate. Fresh, elegant, long and creamy. Lovely balance. **$$$$$ per magnum**

GOLD

Perrier-Jouët Belle Epoque 2007 Blanc (Magnum)
Champagne, France (150cl, 12.50%)
50% Chardonnay, 45% Pinot Noir, 5% Meunier (9g RS)
Stylish super-bright nose with elegant toastiness and soft, lively fruit that is as light as a feather and dances on the palate. Delightful with delicious, zingy fruitiness. **$$$$$ per magnum**

GOLD

Perrier-Jouët Blason NV Rosé
Champagne, France (75cl, 12%)
25% Chardonnay, 50% Meunier, 25% Pinot Noir (10g RS)
Beautiful pale-peach colour, restrained slightly toasty aromas with lovely creamy fruit on palate. Crisp and fruity with a long, creamy finish. Long. **$$$$ per bottle**

GOLD

Perrier-Jouët Blason NV Rosé (Magnum)
Champagne, France (150cl, 12%)
25% Chardonnay, 50% Meunier, 25% Pinot Noir (10g RS)
Pale bronzed-pink colour. Gorgeous, creamy, yeast-complexed, vanilla-dusted red-fruits aromas from start to finish. Lovely fragrant, toast-laden sweet fruitiness caressed by a sumptuous mousse. Crisp, classy and nuanced. **$$$$ per magnum**

SILVER

Perrier-Jouët NV Grand Brut
Champagne, France (75cl, 12%)
20% Chardonnay, 40% Pinot Noir, 40% Meunier (10g RS)
Not complex, but a really enjoyable champagne with a deep, yeast-aged, red-fruit aroma, ample Pinot fruit-driven fruit on a creamy palate and a friendly dosage. **$$$ per bottle**

SILVER

Perrier-Jouët NV Grand Brut (Magnum)
Champagne, France (150cl, 12%)
20% Chardonnay, 40% Meunier, 40% Pinot Noir (10g RS)
Elegant, pretty white fruit aromas, with juicy-sappy fruit with a tropical twist on the palate. Crisp fluffy mousse. Will improve further. **$$$ per magnum**

PIERRE GIMONNET & FILS

SILVER

Pierre Gimonnet 2008 Millésime de Collection (Magnum)
Champagne, France (150cl, 12.50%)
100% Chardonnay (4.5g RS)
Beautifully elegant, gently complex, lush-creamy Chardonnay fruit, with tropical notes, impeccable structure, length and lovely tapering acid-line. Lime after-aromas. **$$$$ per magnum**

SILVER

Pierre Gimonnet 2012 Special Club - Oger Grand Cru
Champagne, France (75cl, 12.50%)
100% Chardonnay (4.5g RS)
Bright yellow-fruit aromas with complexing floral-toasty notes over a streamlined palate of lovely, fresh and elegantly creamy Chardonnay fruit. Harmonious with a long dry finish. **$$$$ per bottle**

PIPER-HEIDSIECK

GOLD

Piper-Heidsieck 2002 Millésime Rare

Champagne, France (75cl, 12.60%)
70% Chardonnay, 30% Pinot Noir (11.1g RS)
Such a soft, friendly and gracefully aged nose with gorgeous, spiced-toast aromas and plenty of yeast-complexed notes. An exquisite toast-laden palate brimming with yeast-complexed, mature, creamy fruit. Smooth, long and lingering with a perfectly judged dosage. **$$$$$ per bottle**

SILVER

Piper-Heidsieck 2006 Vintage

Champagne, France (75cl, 12.70%)
60% Pinot Noir, 40% Chardonnay (9.5g RS)
Soft, rich vanilla-dusted fruit aromas with a touch of dried-fruit oxidativeness and patisserie complexity. Very rich, mellow and yeast-complexed palate. Concentrated with a long vinous finish. Impressive but lacks the elegance required for a Gold. Top Silver. **$$$$ per bottle**

GOLD

Piper-Heidsieck NV Essentiel Cuvée Brut

Champagne, France (75cl, 12.30%)
55% Pinot Noir, 30% Meunier, 15% Chardonnay (6g RS)
This immediately stands out as a classy non-vintage blend, with its impressively toasty aromatics and complexing notes of pastry, dried fruits and spice. Fruity, boosted palate with fresh acidic backbone. Soft, expansive mousse. Long, juicy finish. **$$$$ per bottle**

PLUMPTON ESTATE

GOLD

Plumpton Estate NV The Dean Blush

East Sussex, England (75cl, 12%)
25% Pinot Noir, 30% Meunier, 45% Chardonnay (6g RS)

- Best English NV Rosé

Pale-apricot colour with flecks of onion-skin. Lovely evolved fruit aromas, with fresh, youthful fruit on the palate. Crisp, zingy, spicy, long and focused.
$$$ per bottle

GOLD

Plumpton Estate NV The Dean Brut

England (75cl, 11.50%)
25% Pinot Noir, 30% Meunier, 45% Chardonnay (11g RS)

- Best English NV Blend

Pinot fruit aromas with a hint of tropical fruit and spicy-apple complexing notes. Long, exuberant, fruit-driven. **$$$ per bottle**

POMMERY

GOLD

POMMERY 2003 LES CLOS POMPADOUR MIS EN CAVE 2003 (MAGNUM)
Champagne, France (150cl, 12%)
70% Chardonnay, 25% Pinot Noir, 5% Meunier (9g RS)
- Best Single Vineyard Champagne

Pronounced, expressive nose teeming with a lovely, sulphidic complexity of gunpowder, overlaying great intensity of fine, rich fruit on the palate, with complexing notes of pastry, honey and toast. **$$$$$ per magnum**

SILVER

POMMERY NV BRUT ROYAL (MAGNUM)
Champagne, France (150cl, 12.50%)
34% Chardonnay, 33% Pinot Noir, 33% Meunier (10g RS)
Slow-building toasty aromas over super-fresh, yeast-complexed, succulent fruit driven palate. Seriously superior Silver. Magnum? **$$$ per magnum**

RICCI CURBASTRO

SILVER

RICCI CURBASTRO 2011 EXTRA BRUT
Franciacorta DOCG, Lombardy, Italy (75cl, 12.50%)
50% Chardonnay, 50% Pinot Noir (4g RS)
Very fresh and surprisingly light on its feet for a Franciacorta, this sparkling wine has a lovely white-fruit profile, and a soft yet crisp, creamy palate with an attractive brut finish. **$$$ per bottle**

RIDEGVIEW ESTATE WINERY

GOLD

RIDGEVIEW 2009 ROSÉ DE NOIRS (MAGNUM)
Sussex, England, England (150cl, 12.50%)
63% Meunier, 37% Pinot Noir (10.4g RS)
- Best English Magnum

Light Anjou Rosé colour suggests some development, which is immediately confirmed by its evolving Pinot Noir aromas. Beautifully balanced, gracefully matured, super-long and super-impressive. **$$$$ per magnum**

ROEDERER ESTATE

SILVER

ROEDERER ESTATE 2009 L'ERMITAGE
Anderson Valley AVA, California, USA (75cl, 12%)
52% Chardonnay, 48% Pinot Noir (11g RS)
Creamy, classy and complex, but only just ready to disgorging, hence Silver for what will eventually become a Gold medal sparkling wine. Needs a little cellaring to bring out the full effects of yeast-ageing. **$$$ per bottle**

GOLD

ROEDERER ESTATE NV BRUT (MAGNUM)
Anderson Valley AVA, California, USA (150cl, 12%)
60% Chardonnay, 40% Pinot Noir (12g RS)

- Best California Brut Blend

Pale-lemon colour with bright fruit aromas and lovely satisfying, gentle, yeast-complexed notes. Crisp fruit, super-creamy mousse. **$$$ per magnum**

GOLD

ROEDERER ESTATE NV BRUT ROSÉ (MAGNUM)
Anderson Valley AVA, California, USA (150cl, 12%)
45% Chardonnay, 55% Pinot Noir (12g RS)

- Best California Rosé
- Best California Magnum
- Best US Sparkling Wine

A beautifully pale pink-peach colour. Classy yeast-complexed, toasty-gunflint nose, with bright, gorgeously exuberant fruitiness on a linear palate with a sumptuous mousse and an exquisite acid-line: what more could you ask for? **$$$ per magnum**

ROGER GOULART

SILVER

ROGER GOULART 2013 BRUT RESERVA
Cava DO, Barcelona, Spain (75cl, 12%)
40% Xarel-lo, 30% Macabeo, 30% Parellada (8g RS)
A sleek, modern style of Cava, with a touch of gunpowdery complexity lighting up the fresh and appealing aromatics, followed by a fluffy, succulent palate and a lovely creaminess on long finish. **$$$ per bottle**

ROTARI

GOLD

ROTARI 2010 BLANC DE BLANCS
Trentodoc, Trentino Alto Adige, Italy (75cl, 12.50%)
100% Chardonnay (4g RS)
Refined floral-toasty aromas with notes of crème brulée and apple-pie. This is a fine and super-fresh, classic-structured Chardonnay with lovely, light complexity and text-book dry finish. **$$$ per bottle**

SILVER

ROTARI 2011 RISERVA
Trentodoc, Trentino Alto Adige, Italy (75cl, 12.50%)
100% Chardonnay (8g RS)
A deep, soft, attractively developed, tropical-fruit aroma followed by a lovely energy on the palate, which is intense with a lemony bite and a fine length. This is a refined sparkling win, but a tad fat on the finish and aftertaste, which makes it a great Silver rather than a Gold. **$$$ per bottle**

SILVER

ROTARI ALPEREGIS 2009 PAS DOSÉ

Trentodoc, Trentino Alto Adige, Italy (75cl, 13%)
100% Chardonnay (2g RS)
An opulent, fruit-laden, gently toasty aroma with rapeseed notes. Sunshine in a bottle, creamy mid-palate and a fluffy mousse. **$$$ per bottle**

GOLD

ROTARI ALPEREGIS 2011 ROSÉ

Trentodoc, Trentino Alto Adige, Italy (75cl, 12.50%)
90% Pinot Noir, 10% Chardonnay (7g RS)

- Best Trentodoc Vintaged Rosé

Ultra-pale Roederer-like rosé colour, with gentle gunpowder complexity on the nose and a youthful, silky palate of light and elegant fruit leading to an attractive dry brut finish. **$$$ per bottle**

SILVER

ROTARI CUVÉE 28+ NV ROSÉ

Trentodoc, Trentino Alto Adige, Italy (75cl, 12.50%)
70% Chardonnay, 30% Pinot Noir (7g RS)
Ultra-pale Roederer-like rosé colour, fresh and delicate aroma, quite sweet on the palate, squeaky-clean and quaffing in character. **$$$ per bottle**

GOLD

ROTARI ROSÉ ITALIA NV BRUT ROSÉ

Trentodoc, Trentino Alto Adige, Italy (75cl, 12.50%)
75% Pinot Noir, 25% Chardonnay (7g RS)

- Best Trentodoc NV Rosé
- Best Deluxe Champagne Magnum

Ultra-pale Roederer-like rosé colour, with fresh red-fruit aroma and toasty notes, followed by delicate red-fruits on the palate, carrying through to a good brut finish. Fresh and vibrant. Extremely pleasurable. **$$$ per bottle**

SILVER

ROTARI ROSÉ USA 2013 VINTAGE

Trentodoc, Trentino Alto Adige, Italy (75cl, 12.50%)
75% Pinot Noir, 25% Chardonnay (7g RS)
Ultra-pale Roederer-like rosé colour, pretty and perfumed aroma, crisp, youthful and refreshingly fruit of precision and intensity. **$$$ per bottle**

SILVER

ROTARI USA 2013 BLANC DE BLANCS

Trentodoc, Trentino Alto Adige, Italy (75cl, 12.50%)
100% Chardonnay (6g RS)
Fresh, youthful and elegantly fruity aroma with ample, creamy white-fruit on the palate, long finish and a vanilla aftertaste. **$$$ per bottle**

RUINART

GOLD

Dom Ruinart 2002 Rosé
Champagne, France (75cl, 12.50%)
80% Chardonnay, 20% Pinot Noir (5.5g RS)
Pale-peach colour, with lovely fragrant Pinot aromas, delicate and yet so complex. Firm, zesty and youthful on a classically linear palate, with delightful toasty hints on a beautiful, long finish. **$$$$$ per bottle**

GOLD

Dom Ruinart 2004 Blanc de Blancs
Champagne, France (75cl, 12.50%)
100% Chardonnay (5.5g RS)
Stylish, gunpowder enriched, powerful fruit aromas with complexing notes of vanilla, spice and meadow flower meadows. This is a big, solid, food-style blanc de blancs of obvious class and quality. Nothing linear or tapered her, just full-bodied palate of naked power and a very long, very firm, buttery-burgundian feel. **$$$$$ per bottle**

GOLD

Ruinart NV Blanc de Blancs (Magnum)
Champagne, France (150cl, 12.50%)
100% Chardonnay (9g RS)

- Best Champagne NV Blanc de Blancs
- Best Champagne NV Magnum

Fresh, youthful and zingy, with wonderful fruit, finesse and focus. Deliciously succulent palate of fresh, opulent, bright fruitiness, a long juicy finish and crisp acid backbone. **$$$$ per magnum**

GOLD

Ruinart NV Brut (Magnum)
Champagne, France (150cl, 12%)
50% Pinot Noir, 39% Chardonnay, 11% Meunier (9g RS)
Fresh, yeast-complexed fruit aromas with complexing notes of toast, vanilla and pastry. Plush and fruity on the palate. A classy, seamless, polished wine with stand-out magnum effect to smooth the mousse. **$$$$ per magnum**

GOLD

Ruinart NV Rosé (Magnum)
Champagne, France (150cl, 12.50%)
55% Pinot Noir, 45% Chardonnay (9g RS)
Young pink-bronze colour. Clean and expressive fruity aromas dominated by pencil-shaving notes of evolving Pinot fruitiness. Vinous, fleshy, soothing palate. Long and full of lovely fruit. So juicy! **$$$$ per magnum**

SCHARFFENBERGER CELLARS

SILVER

Scharffenberger NV Excellence Brut
Mendocino County AVA, California, USA (75cl, 12%)
60% Chardonnay, 40% Pinot Noir (9g RS)
Mid-lemon colour. Opulent, creamy-toasty aroma with vanilla and pastry complexity. Creamy palate with succulent fruit-acidity and a satisfying brut balance. **$$ per bottle**

SCHLOSS GOBELSBURG

SILVER

Schloss Gobelsburg NV Brut Réserve
Niederösterreich, Niederösterreich, Austria (75cl, 12%)
70% Grüner Veltliner, 15% Pinot Noir, 15% Riesling (8g RS)
Mid-lemon colour. Elegant, restrained, spiced-fruit aroma with floral and waxy notes. Fine, lengthy and broad on the palate, with fruit tapering nicely to a distinctly crisp and dry finish. Good minerality. **$$$ per bottle**

SCHLUMBERGER

SILVER

Schlumberger 2013 Rosé Brut
Austria (75cl, 11.50%)
100% Pinot Noir (10g RS)
Pale pink colour. Soft and sweet berry nose with crisp, clean, highly singular red-fruit on the palate. Quite elegant with soft brut finish. **$$ per bottle**

SEGURA VIUDAS

GOLD

Segura Viudas 2011 Vintage Gran Reserva
Cava DO, Spain (75cl, 12%)
67% Macabeo, 33% Parellada (3g RS)
- Best Low or No Dosage Cava

Mid-lemon colour. Lovely aged vanilla depth. Fine fruitiness on a fluffy mousse. Beautifully made, sleek, elegant and pristine with a long, long tapering finish. Gorgeous mousse and finish. **$$ per bottle**

GOLD

Segura Viudas NV Brut Reserva
Cava DO, Spain (75cl, 12%)
50% Macabeo, 35% Parellada, 15% Xarel-lo (9g RS)
Pale-lemon-green colour. Very fresh and young, with a recently disgorged, spicy aroma. Sweet for a brut, but beautifully smooth integration of the three varietals with absolutely pristine fruit. Linear and driven. **$$ per bottle**

GOLD

SEGURA VIUDAS NV GRAN CUVÉE RESERVA
Cava DO, Spain (75cl, 12%)
70% Macabeo, 15% Parellada, 10% Chardonnay, 5% Pinot Noir (6g RS)
Pale-lemon-green colour. Fresh yellow fruit aromas with notes of toast and charred-spice followed by fresh and zingy fruit on the palate. **$$ per bottle**

SILVER

SEGURA VIUDAS NV RESERVA HEREDAD ROSÉ
Cava DO, Spain (75cl, 12%)
100% Pinot Noir, None (9g RS)
Gorgeous, Roederer-like, ultra-pale-salmon colour. Fresh and delicate peach aroma with heaps of fruit on the palate, which is just so very long with an incredibly indelible finish. Super top Silver! **$$$ per bottle**

SEKTHAUS SOLTER

SILVER

SOLTER RHEINGAU RIESLING SEKT 2005 RÉSERVE
Berg Roseneck, Rheingau, Germany (75cl, 12.50%)
100% Riesling (5.3g RS)
Deep golden colour. Developed Riesling aroma complex notes of honey, wax, spice and apricot. Very fresh palate. Long, strong finish. **$$$ per bottle**

SQUERRYEYS

GOLD

SQUERRYES 2011 BRUT
Kent, England (75cl, 12%)
45% Chardonnay, 35% Pinot Noir, 20% Meunier (10.5g RS)

- Best English Vintaged Blend
- Best Value English Sparkling Wine
- Best English Sparkling Wine

What lovely, satisfying, linear wine this is. Bright fruit aromas, fine, focused yeast-complexed fruit on the palate, which is as clean as a whistle, with a lovely, fluffy mousse and a laser-like finish. It is fair to say that we were all totally surprised by the National Trophy result as soon as we discovered its identity, but we were equally as pleased as punch that yet another new English sparkling wine name has hit the heights. **$$$ per bottle**

TAITTINGER

GOLD

TAITTINGER 2009 BRUT
Champagne, France (75cl, 12.50%)
50% Chardonnay, 50% Pinot Noir (9g RS)
Lovely, delicate fruity aroma with very little evolution evident, suggesting exceptional longevity. Fresh floral notes over peach and ripe yellow apple. Citrussy crisp palate, long and creamy finish. **$$$$ per bottle**

GOLD

TAITTINGER COMTES DE CHAMPAGNE 2006 BLANC DE BLANCS BRUT
Champagne, France (75cl, 12.50%)
100% Chardonnay (9g RS)

- Best Deluxe Champagne Blanc de Blancs

Truly beautiful, totally classic, extremely high class blanc de blancs. Light, elegant perfumed-floral aroma with a lovely toasty kick. Coffee, vanilla and pure white fruits. Feather-light and fluffy palate, very clean fruitiness smooth-textured, balanced finish and gentle acidity. ***$$$$$ per bottle***

SILVER

TAITTINGER NV BRUT RÉSERVE
Champagne, France (75cl, 12.50%)
40% Chardonnay, 35% Pinot Noir, 25% Meunier (9g RS)
Clean, youthful, white-fruit aroma with complex notes of peach, melon and yeast-aged candied richness. Lovely, fresh, well-balanced, elegantly fruit-driven, creamy palate with a long, linear, juicy, silky finish. **$$$ per bottle**

GOLD

TAITTINGER NV FOLIES DE LA MARQUETTERIE
Champagne, France (75cl, 12.50%)
55% Pinot Noir, 45% Chardonnay (9g RS)
Soft, fresh, floral-fruit aromas, very youthful with little yeast-complexing evident. Fresh and succulent on the palate, which is classy and Pinot-dominated, with sweet, peachy, yeast-complexed Chardonnay undertones. Long, with a mouth-watering juicy finish. **$$$$ per bottle**

SILVER

TAITTINGER NV PRÉLUDE GRANDS CRUS
Champagne, France (75cl, 12.50%)
50% Chardonnay, 50% Pinot Noir (9g RS)
Lovely soft white-fruit aroma with complexing peach notes layered over toast. Crisp, fluffy and fleshy fruit on a well-structured, creamy palate. Sweet, juicy and long. **$$$$ per bottle**

TALTARNI VINEYARDS

SILVER

TALTARNI 2011 CUVÉE ROSÉ
South East Australia, Australia (75cl, 11.70%)
60% Chardonnay, 30% Pinot Noir, 10% Meunier (6.3g RS)
Very, very pale, copper-hued colour, with refined aromatics showing some age-derived complexity. Very young fruit on the palate, which is soft and caressing. Mature after notes. **$$ per bottle**

TENUTA DEGLI ULTIMI

GOLD

Tenuta Degli Ultimi 2013 Rive di Collalto Biancariva
Conegliano-Valdobbiadene Prosecco Superiore DOCG (Rive), Veneto, Italy (75cl, 11.50%)
88% Glera, 10% Bianchetta, 2% Verdiso (5g RS)

- Best Prosecco Low or No Dosage

Attractive white fruit aroma with spicy, estery notes. Surprisingly fresh for what is by Prosecco terms a relatively mature wine. The fruit on the palate is soft and round, and tastes sweeter than it actually is (just 5g), with a long juicy finish. **$$ per bottle**

THE CO-OPERATIVE

SILVER

Les Pionniers 2006 Vintage Champagne
Champagne, France (75cl, 12%)
50% Pinot Noir, 50% Chardonnay (9.1g RS)
Evolved, ample fruity aromas with complex notes of pastry and nuttiness. Soft, creamy and fleshy on the palate. Needs more time. **$$$ per bottle**

THIÉNOT

GOLD

Thiénot 2008 Vintage
Champagne, France (75cl, 12.50%)
40% Chardonnay, 35% Meunier, 25% Pinot Noir (10g RS)
Discreetly fruity-floral aroma, very pretty and squeaky-clean, with notes of peach and toast. Gentle, charming and elegant palate, with a sweet, crisp and energising finish. **$$$ per bottle**

SILVER

Thiénot NV Brut
Champagne, France (75cl, 12.50%)
45% Chardonnay, 35% Pinot Noir, 20% Meunier (10g RS)
Fine, fresh and youthful red-fruit aromas with some spicy, yeast-aged complexity. Full and intense, but more Silver than Gold. **$$$ per bottle**

TÖRLEY

SILVER

Törley NV Fortuna
Etyek-Buda, Hungary (75cl, 6.60%)
40% Moscato, 30% Cserszegi Fűszeres, 30% Csabagyöngye (66g RS)
Pale-lemon colour. Grapey and floral with a touch of Moscato, a super-soft mousse and long, fresh and balanced sweetness on the finish. **$ per bottle**

UBERTI

GOLD

UBERTI 2008 COMARÌ DEL SALEM (MAGNUM)
Franciacorta DOCG, Lombardy, Italy (150cl, 13.50%)
80% Chardonnay, 20% Pinot Bianco (3g RS)

- Best Low or No Dosage Franciacorta

Super-stylish, toast-complexed nose, with gorgeous, slow-evolving vanilla-dusted toasty fruit. Creamy and long. Classy. **$$$$ per magnum**

GOLD

UBERTI QUINQUE CUVÉE DI 5 VENDEMMIE NV EXTRA BRUT (MAGNUM)
Franciacorta DOCG, Lombardy, Italy (150cl, 13.30%)
100% Chardonnay (3g RS)
Gunpowder-toastiness on nose and palate. Mellow yeast and toast complexed ripe fruits on the palate. Lovely soft mousse. **$$$$ per magnum**

ULYSSE COLLIN

SILVER

ULYSSE COLLIN NV LES ROISES BLANC DE BLANCS
Champagne, France (75cl, 12%)
100% Chardonnay (3g RS)
Full-on toasty-oak-powered aroma with vanilla, tropical fruit and yeast-aged, spicy complexity. Rich, sumptuous, vanilla-toned Chardonnay fruit on a soft, creamy palate with a fluffy mousse. **$$$$ per bottle**

VEUVE CLICQUOT

GOLD

VEUVE CLICQUOT 2008 VINTAGE
Champagne, France (75cl, 12%)
61% Pinot Noir, 34% Chardonnay, 5% Meunier (8g RS)
Magic! Perfect balance. Pulsing with fine energy and freshness. Ten years away from approaching its peak. **$$$$ per bottle**

GOLD

VEUVE CLICQUOT 2008 VINTAGE ROSÉ
Champagne, France (75cl, 12%)
76% Pinot Noir, 21% Chardonnay, 3% Meunier (8g RS)
Medium-salmon colour. Perfumed aromas with spice-laden notes. Extremely Pinot-driven. Fresh and smart. Classic tight 2008 finish. **$$$$ per bottle**

SILVER

VEUVE CLICQUOT NV VEUVE CLICQUOT ROSÉ
Champagne, France (75cl, 12%)
62% Pinot Noir, 15% Meunier, 23% Chardonnay (10g RS)
Youthful peach colour. Yeast-complexed, fruity aroma, with red-fruits and chalkiness on the palate, carrying well to a dry finish. **$$$$ per bottle**

SILVER

VEUVE CLICQUOT NV YELLOW LABEL
Champagne, France (75cl, 12%)
50% Pinot Noir, 20% Meunier, 30% Chardonnay (10g RS)
Mellow, creamy, yeast-complexed aromas, with notes of baking spices and spiced-apple. Brisk palate with good energy. Well-balanced. **$$$ per bottle**

SILVER

VEUVE CLICQUOT NV YELLOW LABEL (MAGNUM)
Champagne, France (150cl, 12%)
50% Pinot Noir, 20% Meunier, 30% Chardonnay (10g RS)
Young, long and soft, this shows great elegance for a well-structured style, with a lovely mousse, and juicy fruit on the finish. A stunning Silver for a very classy Champagne that can only improve in bottle. **$$$$ per magnum**

VILARNAU

GOLD

VILARNAU NV BRUT RESERVA
Cava DO, Spain (75cl, 11.50%)
50% Macabeo, 35% Parellada, 15% Xarel-lo (10g RS)
- Best Cava NV Brut Blend

Pale-lemon in colour, with gunpowder-toast. The fruit on the palate is plush, early-picked and caressed by a soft cushiony mousse. Smart winemaking. **$$ per bottle**

VILLA SANDI

SILVER

OPERE TREVIGIANE NV METODO TRADIZIONALE
Serenissima DOC, Veneto, Italy (75cl, 12%)
60% Chardonnay, 40% Pinot Noir (10g RS)
Fresh, crisp and youthful white-fruit aroma with light but impressive complexity. Classic structured palate, creamy mousse. **$ per bottle**

SILVER

VILLA SANDI NV CUVÉE ORIS
Valdobbiadene Prosecco Superiore DOCG, Veneto, Italy (75cl, 11.50%)
100% Glera (21g RS)
Soft and delicate peardrop aromas, with fresh, pure fruit and a super-fine mousse on the palate. Light-bodied, easy to drink and not too sweet. **$$ per bottle**

WAITROSE

GOLD

WAITROSE 2005 SPECIAL RÉSERVE VINTAGE
Champagne, France (75cl, 12.50%)
50% Chardonnay, 41% Pinot Noir, 9% Meunier (10g RS)

- Best Supermarket Champagne
- Best Value Champagne

Soft, yeast-complexed aroma with charred, vanilla, toast and white-fruit notes. Full and soft and caressingly smooth on the palate. **$$$ per bottle**

WILDEKRANS WINE ESTATE

SILVER

WILDEKRANS 2013 CHENIN BLANC

Cap Classique, Botriver, Western Cape, South Africa (75cl, 13%)
100% Chenin Blanc (10.5g RS)
Distinctive varietal aroma with a floral expression, crisp palate, ripe fruit profile, with spiced-vanilla complexity and fine length. Good to see a serious sparkling wine made from South Africa's esteemed Chenin Blanc, especially when it is well worth a Silver medal. **$$ per bottle**

WISTON ESTATE

GOLD

WISTON ESTATE 2010 BLANC DE BLANCS

South Downs, England (75cl, 12%)
100% Chardonnay (8g RS)

- Best English Blanc de Blancs

Yeast-complexed, bright, fruity aromas with lovely, satisfying, linear fruit on the palate. Big, fluffy mouse. Clean as a whistle with a laser-like finish. English winemaking at its finest. **$$$ per bottle**

SILVER

WISTON ESTATE 2010 BLANC DE NOIRS

South Downs, England (75cl, 12%)
70% Pinot Noir, 25% Meunier, 5% Chardonnay (9g RS)
Very fine, super-pure Pinot fruit (even though it contains 5% Chardonnay) aromas follow through onto the palate, which is crisp, intense and fully of crunchy red-fruit flavour. Very linear, with a tight acid-line. **$$$ per bottle**

Printed in Great Britain
by Amazon